"As Christians increasingly join in the cause of social justice, it's a good time to remember that people of faith have always joined—and often led—great reform movements. Tim Stafford helps us pause, reflect and learn from both the wisdom and folly of that colorful past."

PHILIP YANCEY

"Many of America's great social movements—abolition, temperance, women's suffrage, civil rights—had their roots in the Christian faith. In his thoughtful and eminently practical analysis of these movements, Tim Stafford counsels would-be Christian activists in how to be 'as shrewd as snakes and as innocent as doves.' I especially appreciate his take on the role of truth for activists who seek to be both passionate and durable. Although to most of our postmodern sensibilities truth has been relativized to be non-consequential, Stafford reminds us that the truth of God's kingdom insists on activism and social change. *Shaking the System* is an 'ebenezer,' recounting how God has worked redemptively in America's past, and how God can work again today."

RUSSELL JEUNG, ASSOCIATE PROFESSOR OF ASIAN AMERICAN STUDIES, SAN FRANCISCO STATE UNIVERSITY, AUTHOR AND ASIAN AMERICAN CHRISTIAN ACTIVIST

"Insightful, probing reflection on Christian activist struggles to change America. Wisely cautionary, firmly encouraging. A must-read for all activists who want to change the world."

RONALD J. SIDER, PRESIDENT, EVANGELICALS FOR SOCIAL ACTION

"*Shaking the System* is a brilliant analysis of Christian attempts at needed social reforms, heavily focused on the abolitionist and civil rights movements. This is not a romantic or idealistic analysis, but it is brutally realistic about the pitfalls and problems as well as the limited successes of these movements. Very few white evangelicals write with the insight and wisdom of Stafford."

JOHN PERKINS, JOHN PERKINS FOUNDATION

"It is deeply gratifying to see one of contemporary evangelicalism's most eloquent and respected thinkers plumb the wisdom of the great reform movements of American history. *Shaking the System* is a passionate and riveting account of Christian faith in action. Tim Stafford tells stories that inspire acts of courage and compassion, and at the same time, he shows us why courage and compassion must be grounded in costly discipleship to Jesus Christ. This book has the power to renew Christian social witness in our time."

CHARLES MARSH, AUTHOR OF *THE BELOVED COMMUNITY* AND DIRECTOR OF THE PROJECT ON LIVED THEOLOGY, UNIVERSITY OF VIRGINIA

"Activists (especially Christian activists) are too often unaware of our own history. Tim Stafford tells us that history—from the abolition of slavery to women's suffrage to civil rights—and draws from it the important lessons for today. This is an important handbook for a new generation, and a welcome refresher for those who have been in the struggle for years. He closes with the most important reminder—that what ultimately calls us into activism is the kingdom of God breaking into our world. We are motivated not by partisan politics but by the message of Jesus. I heartily recommend *Shaking the System* to all those who seek both a deeper faithfulness and a better world."

JIM WALLIS, AUTHOR OF *GOD'S POLITICS,* AND PRESIDENT, SOJOURNERS

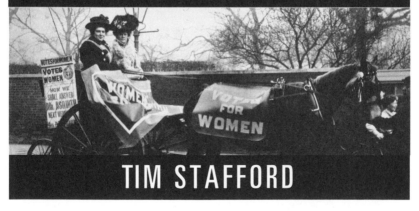

SHAKING THE SYSTEM

What I Learned from the Great American Reform Movements

TIM STAFFORD

IVP Books

An imprint of InterVarsity Press
Downers Grove, Illinois

InterVarsity Press
P.O. Box 1400, Downers Grove, IL 60515-1426
World Wide Web: www.ivpress.com
E-mail: email@ivpress.com

InterVarsity Press® is the book-publishing division of InterVarsity Christian Fellowship/USA®, a student movement active on campus at hundreds of universities, colleges and schools of nursing in the United States of America, and a member movement of the International Fellowship of Evangelical Students. For information about local and regional activities, write Public Relations Dept., InterVarsity Christian Fellowship/USA, 6400 Schroeder Rd., P.O. Box 7895, Madison, WI 53707-7895, or visit the IVCF website at <www.intervarsity.org>.

Design: Cindy Kiple
Images: Rev. Martin Luther King Jr. and Freedom Riders: Time Life Pictures/Getty Images
        The Great Anti-Slavery Meeting of 1841: The Bridgeman Art Library/Getty Images
        Votes for women press cart: The Bridgeman Art Library/Getty Images

ISBN 978-0-8308-3436-5

Printed in the United States of America ∞

Library of Congress Cataloging-in-Publication Data

Stafford, Tim, 1950-
   Shaking the system: what I learned from the great American reform
   movements / Tim Stafford.
      p. cm.
   Includes bibliographical references and index.
   ISBN 978-0-8308-3436-5 (cloth: alk. paper)
   1. United States—Church history. 2. Church and social
   problems—United States. I. Title.
   BR517.S58 2007
   261.8'30973—dc22

                                                                            2007021664

| P | 19 | 18 | 17 | 16 | 15 | 14 | 13 | 12 | 11 | 10 | 9 | 8 | 7 | 6 | 5 | 4 | 3 | 2 | 1 |
| Y | 23 | 22 | 21 | 20 | 19 | 18 | 17 | 16 | 15 | 14 | 13 | 12 | 11 | 10 | 09 | 08 | 07 | | | |

CONTENTS

HOW DO WE CHANGE THE WORLD?

I CAME OF AGE IN AN ERA OF RECKLESS IDEALISM, when war in Vietnam was causing immense turmoil in America. It was a time of marches, sit-ins, draft-card burnings and all manner of protests. During my freshman year of college, I found myself in an eleven-day sit-in at a university research lab, protesting secret research done for the Defense Department.

I got involved without much thought. The resident assistant in my freshman dorm was an idealistic and passionate Christian, and he accosted me and several of my friends, urging us to join in the protest. Hardly knowing what it was about, I went along. Students had just occupied the building of the Applied Electronics Laboratory—a place I had never seen, buried in a remote corner of the campus. I had not thought about the question of secret research, but I knew I hated the war.

For almost two weeks, I was among several hundred students who studied at the laboratory, slept there and held passionate, extended meetings to vote on tactics. A photograph of me studying my calculus text while sitting on the lab floor ended up on the front page of a Stanford alumni newspaper, and through that photograph my parents learned what I was doing. Years later my sisters told me that my father cried when he saw it. His tears frightened them much more than his loud denunciations.

Our protest ended when the university agreed to end all secret research. We were jubilant—and relieved. We had expected to be arrested. Instead we had changed the direction of a great university. Before we left the building, we carefully tidied it, anxious to demonstrate that we were not destructive. Those were the early, innocent days of protest.

The university's secret research stopped, but the war in Vietnam did not. I participated in other protests and never changed my mind that war was an evil disaster. However, I was never again on the front lines of a radical demonstration. The sit-in had made me a little edgy about involvement. While participating in endless meetings, I gradually became aware that this was not such a simple exercise in grass-roots democracy as it seemed. Some of our leaders—older and more experienced, in most cases—had an unspoken agenda. For them, our sit-in was just the first stage in a campaign to radicalize the university. They had deep and wide leftist commitments, but they didn't say so to freshmen like me. I began to understand, rather dimly, how a protest movement can be manipulated. I didn't like the sense of being used, and it made me wary of involvement where I wasn't quite sure about the leaders' deeper agenda.

Joining a movement is like jumping into a fast-moving river. You find out that the river has a momentum of its own.

As it turned out, what began as peaceful protests became quite violent within a year's time. I suspect that the situation ran away even from those who had hoped to radicalize the university. Some people had a genuine taste for throwing rocks and smashing windows. They showed up at every event. Nobody could control them. Increasingly I stayed away.

Three years later I was canvassing door-to-door for George McGovern's presidential campaign. That was antiwar activism, too, but of a different kind. It was not notably successful. McGovern lost the election in a landslide to Richard Nixon.

It seemed the war in Vietnam would never end. Its horrible futility and its even more hideous death toll made me depressed and sick, as though I had a fever that wouldn't go away. The military draft awaited me when I left college, as it awaited all my male friends. Could it really happen that I would be forced to kill—and be killed—for a cause I didn't understand, let alone believe in? I talked to a "draft counselor," but I couldn't convince myself that I was a genuine conscientious objector. I would fight for my country if the fight seemed just. But fighting in this war, an aimless nightmare—I couldn't imagine it.

I wanted to stop the war. But how to do it?

★   ★   ★

I remember talking to a college pastor, a man I greatly respected. He was a kind person, not quick to voice disapproval, but all his gentleness couldn't conceal the fact that he took a dim view of my involvement in student protests. He thought they stirred up trouble and distracted me from the real issues. Those real issues, he believed, came down to witnessing to your faith. "The world isn't going to change until people change," he told me. "Until they know the Lord, people couldn't change even if they wanted to. If enough people become Christians, they will have an impact on society."

There is something to what my pastor friend said. When Christian faith spreads broadly in a society, it has a deep social impact.

And surely the world can't change profoundly unless people are transformed deep at heart.

But, I wondered, is the choice really one or the other—activism or Christian witness? Isn't it possible that more people will receive our witness if they see us actively caring about injustice? Why couldn't I witness to Jesus as I carried on protesting the war?

My pastor was quite sincere in what he said. But I think his either-or perspective concealed a conviction that changing the world either wasn't truly important or wasn't truly possible. His basic approach was to rescue as many sinners as possible from a dying world and to hold on until the return of Jesus.

I wasn't happy just to hold on. I couldn't accept that we had to carry on an insane war until enough people became Christians to bring peace on earth. I knew the world wouldn't become like heaven through my activism, but I thought it might become a better place.

★   ★   ★

The war did finally end, but the sleepy contentment of pre-Vietnam America never returned. Activism had been awakened. Some organized fiercely for women's liberation and the sexual revolution. Utopian communes were launched, including many based on Christian beliefs as well as others based on marijuana. César Chávez led farm worker demonstrations. The civil rights movement led to the Black Panthers. The first small protests against legalized abortion began, which would lead to decades of social and political strife, still unresolved today.

A lot of such activism fizzled. Most of my peers settled down to make money, raise a family and play golf. And yet, the age of activism persisted. Today it is impossible to live in America without encountering idealists who march, organize, accost you at the supermarket seeking contributions or signatures, write letters to the editor, organize neighborhood committees, post blogs and speak in our places of worship. They appeal to our idealism, asking us to join them or at least to support them with our money and votes.

I thank God for such activists, even when I don't agree with them. I know that the world needs their passion. Even more, *I* need it. They keep me awake to a world in pain. We need activism because the world needs to change for the better. It will not change if everybody is content to stay home fixing up the house or playing video games.

Just as much, though, we need wisdom lest passionate convictions lead to silliness or social chaos. The history of activism shows that fervent people often burn out or create unintended consequences. Protest movements get hijacked. Grand efforts turn soggy and fall apart like wet Kleenex. To change the world, our lives and our plans need to be constructed with care.

I certainly apply that to myself. Here are some of the "activism" activities I have tried:

- For years I volunteered once a week at the Catholic Worker soup kitchen.
- My wife and I spent four years in Africa, where I helped to start a magazine for young people by setting up systems and training staff.
- I serve on the mission committee of my church, which supports all kinds of good causes among the poor around the world.
- I serve on the board of a nonprofit organization that helps majority-world pastors to get training.

- I write letters to Congress.
- I served on a neighborhood committee that worked to preserve a green space near my home.
- I put up lawn signs to support local politicians.
- I write letters to the editor of my local newspaper.
- I try to get writing assignments that allow me to encourage causes for justice. For example, I recently wrote a piece on a food emergency in Kenya, and I did another on the Christian Community Development Association (CCDA).
- For years I made a special point of praying daily for a peaceful end to apartheid in South Africa.

I don't know whether that list strikes you as substantial. To me, it seems very flimsy. Other priorities—mainly job and family—have dominated. I can serve good causes through my work as a writer, but it doesn't feel nearly as altruistic as serving meals at the soup kitchen or marching in a protest. I haven't done much, I feel. Nevertheless, I continue to care about changing the world. And I wonder how best to do it.

I am no expert. I am more of a seeker. In that, I am not alone. I meet many young people who want to make a difference in the world. And not just young people—grandparents too.

The plight of people with AIDS cries out for activism. So does world hunger. Issues like abortion, environmental degradation, gay marriage, globalization, genetically modified foods, immigration and many others mobilize activists on one side or another.

In fact, many people are impatient. They don't want to reflect and philosophize about what to do. They figure the problems of the world are so demanding, they better get on with it. Grab a hammer, they seem to say—let's go build something. Or knock something down.

It's not really that simple. Sooner or later you have to think about the best way to make a difference. On almost any issue, different activists have chosen different pathways.

HIV/AIDS

As one example, consider HIV/AIDS, the worldwide plague that decimates whole populations. You can follow many different models for getting involved in the fight against AIDS.

Radical civil disobedience. ACT UP was formed in 1987 by Larry Kramer and a group of about three hundred activists who felt that bolder political action was needed. Highly confrontational, they chose tactics that soon became notorious. One time they partly occupied the trading floor of the New York Stock Exchange and hung in effigy the commissioner of the Federal Drug Administration. Their disgust with Cardinal John O'Connor led some members to interrupt mass at Saint Patrick's Cathedral in New York, throwing condoms at the altar and chanting slogans during the service. The Seattle branch distributed "safer sex" packets at Seattle schools, complete with a graphically illustrated pamphlet titled "How to F*** Safely." There's no doubt ACT UP brought attention to the crisis of HIV/AIDS, though they also fueled negative reactions.

Making noise and friends. Bono, lead singer of the rock band U2, shows an equal flair for the dramatic, but he goes out of his way to make friends, not enemies. In 2002 he met with U.S. President George W. Bush to discuss world poverty and to stand by him at a press conference announcing a new aid effort. At a 2006 National Prayer Breakfast, Bono praised Bush (who would follow him to the platform) for increasing aid to the African continent. Bono was criticized by activists who consider Bush the archenemy.

Bono consistently refuses to draw hard lines between allies and enemies. His way is to use his celebrity to draw attention to humanitarian causes, HIV/AIDS among them, and pull others in. He starts organizations, leads crusades, participates in benefit concerts and recordings, and tries to bring international pressure to politicians. He can be very critical, naming names of those he believes have failed. For example, he publicly criticized Canadian prime minister Paul Martin when he believed Martin had failed to increase foreign aid as he ought to have done. And he has spoken critically of the church's passivity. Generally, though, Bono's style of activism emphasizes making noise and making friends—building coalitions and generating support for good deeds. Few people have his star power, but many activists take the same approach in a more limited, local sense.

Grass-roots care. But isn't it better to go directly to the root of the problem? A friend of mine, Arlene Cummins, has served as a nurse in remote Kenyan hospitals for the past twenty-five years. She is invisible to the media, but undoubtedly she grapples with the HIV/AIDS crisis in a way that Bono and ACT UP never can. She doesn't post pictures of needy children on the Internet; she cares for them face-to-face.

All over the world, you find people like Arlene serving the poor and giving their lives to help them. In a South African slum, I met women who take in children orphaned by AIDS, even though they themselves live in shacks and hardly have enough to feed their own children. In West Africa, a young family friend is working with regional health programs, doing the unglamorous task of researching and implementing best practices in the sometimes stifling medical bureaucracy. Go to Africa, Asia, Latin America or any big city and you will find opportunities to care for those infected with HIV/AIDS and to help prevent its transmission. You can spoon food into the mouths of weak or dying patients, clean the homes of families that are unable to care for themselves, teach abstinence to teenagers, distribute condoms to truck drivers, and any number of other actions. If you have the skills, you can join in the gigantic endeavor to find a vaccine for HIV/AIDS by working in a laboratory.

If you are passionate about HIV/AIDS, what way should you go? Angry street protests are worlds apart from working in a clinic in Uganda. Benefit rock concerts for HIV/AIDS have little in common with bathing someone who can no longer get out of bed to go to the bathroom. If you jump into this river, where will the current carry you?

WAR

Take war as another example. I hope that the war in Iraq will have ended by the time you read this, but at the moment it is a potent example of an activist's choices. When the war first started, I was bombarded with e-mails from an activist friend supporting an initiative by Christian Peacemaker Teams (CPT). CPT is an organization founded by Mennonites, Quakers and Brethren, traditional churches of peace. CPT is dedicated to putting nonviolent volunteers into crisis locations. The idea is to put your body between the warring parties and plead directly for peace. Despite the danger, CPT sent a team into Iraq. Four of their members were kidnapped and held captive for months; one, Tom Fox, was killed.

CPT and a similar organization, Peace Brigades International, send teams into trouble spots all over the world, such as the civil

war in Sri Lanka, the guerilla conflict in Colombia and even hos-
tilities at Wounded Knee, South Dakota.

You can oppose war in less risky ways, of course. A group of
women in a town near my home wear black and stand silently on
a central street at noon every day. An almost ninety-year-old friend
of mine, a Catholic nun, walked miles through sleet and rain while
participating in a Philadelphia march against the Iraq war.

Others employ more conventional political activism. They work
for specific candidates who take a stand against the war. They believe that politics got the United States into Iraq and politics will
get us out of it, so the strongest statements will be made in voting
booths.

WORLD POVERTY

Poverty is a less controversial subject, but that doesn't make it simple. Almost everybody claims to want to help the poor, but what is
the best way to do that? Years ago I wrote a profile on Ron Sider, a
seminary professor who earned his doctorate from Yale. Though a
dedicated teacher, he has made world poverty his lifelong cause. He
writes books, including his best-known *Rich Christians in an Age of
Hunger;* he leads an activist organization called Evangelicals for Social Action; and he gets involved in almost any nationwide Christian initiative that targets poverty. Sider is soft-spoken, friendly and
sensible, but he has shown tremendous staying power through
more than thirty years of activism. Even though Sider's moderate
liberal politics are miles from the religious right, he works hard to
build bridges with Christian conservatives. Like Bono, his approach is to make noise and to make friends. Year after year he
hangs in there, not terribly splashy but incredibly persistent.

Another persistent friend of mine is Alan Doswald, an activist who founded and runs Evangelicals for Social Action (unrelated to Sider's group) in Fresno, California, where I grew up. Doswald has focused on doing good at a practical, grass-roots level. His group helps Fresno churches organize to help the poor in their immediate vicinity.

Doswald and his colleagues have made a tremendous difference. I've never seen a place where Christians from so many different churches work together in practical ways to help their neighbors. Doswald is nonpolitical and nonconfrontational. He appeals to churches' core beliefs, talking their language of love and concern. His group is resolutely local, while Sider's work is mainly national.

In certain ways, Doswald reminds me of John Perkins. Perkins is an African American man who grew up under segregation in rural Mississippi. He held his dying brother Clyde in his arms after Clyde was shot by a trigger-happy police officer. As an angry and embittered teenager, Perkins got out of the South and went west to California, where—though he had never finished elementary school—he succeeded through hard work and sheer ability. Then, just when his life was going well, he became a Christian.

Perkins became convinced that God wanted him to take his faith back to Mississippi. In 1960 he and his wife and children returned to the rural South, where Perkins dedicated his life to preaching the gospel and helping poor African American communities. He was jailed and beaten by a white establishment that feared losing control of "their" blacks. The black community was not uniformly supportive either. Yet Perkins and his wife, Vera Mae, made a mark on communities that had drifted along helplessly for generations. Perkins's work was also resolutely local, but it has had a national impact as he inspired a generation of activists who learned of his work.

Millard Fuller is a completely different kind of character—a wild entrepreneur, a visionary. He made a fortune in business as a young man in Montgomery, Alabama. Then, after selling everything and giving the money away, Fuller and his wife found their way to a radical Christian commune in rural Georgia.

Fuller got involved in building housing for the poor black farmers in the area. Eventually he set up an organization, Habitat for Humanity. Working from a small town in rural Georgia, starting with no money and very few powerful contacts, he made Habitat the biggest homebuilder in the world.

So which approach does the most good? National coalition-building with political overtones? A local program connecting churches to poor people? Community development that serves as a national model? Or using volunteers to do something practical about an issue such as housing?

Or should you fight global poverty more confrontationally? One friend of mine has spent the last two years with International Justice Ministries in India, cajoling the police into raiding businesses that literally enslave their workers.

Another friend feels great concern for the politics of globalization. When the World Trade Organization came to Seattle in 1999, she was on the streets. Massive and occasionally violent protests caused the meetings to fail. Though my friend didn't approve of the violence, she looked on those obstructive protests as a success.

ABORTION

When the Supreme Court declared in 1973 that restrictions on abortion are unconstitutional, it set off protests that continue to this day. For years, a daring, confrontational tactic advocated by activist Randall Terry was at the top of the news. Terry spoke of "rescues." Groups of nonviolent protestors would march unannounced to an abortion clinic and plead with the people coming and going not to partake in abortion. Sometimes they would block access to the clinics.

On the first Friday in May 1990, an envelope came to the door of Randy Alcorn's semirural home in Gresham, Oregon, east of Portland. Inside the envelope was a copy of a writ of garnishment for Alcorn's wages. The writ required Good Shepherd Church, where Alcorn was pastor of missions, to surrender a portion of his wages.

Alcorn instantly understood the reason for the order. In 1989 Portland police had arrested him for blocking the doors of several abortion clinics. One of the clinics had sued him and other "rescuers," winning a small judgment plus attorney's fees. Alcorn had refused to pay, believing it would violate his conscience to write a check to an abortion clinic.

Before the suit, Alcorn and his wife, Nanci, had placed all their assets in her name—the house, car and bank account. Alcorn had given away or sold the copyrights to his five published books. At a debtor's hearing, he was able to state truthfully that he owned nothing of value. An opposing lawyer went so far as to ask about the gold band he was wearing on his left hand. Alcorn held up the ring, milking the drama of the moment. "I'm not sure what it's worth today," he said, "but I paid $12.50 for it at Kmart four years ago."

But Alcorn had not anticipated having his wages garnished. This implicated not just his own conscience, but also that of his church. If the church refused to pay, serious legal consequences could follow. Many church members already had grave doubts about the wisdom of Alcorn's protests, and now they could be sucked into the backwash.

Quickly Alcorn resigned his pastorate. After spending some time praying and strategizing, he and his wife registered a non-profit organization called Eternal Perspectives Ministry. There he would work earning minimum wage, writing and speaking and facilitating global mission causes. His wife would also work there as a part-time secretary while taking care of their two children. The Alcorns lived frugally so they could survive on the very low salaries paid by such jobs.

Since that day, Randy Alcorn has literally owned nothing and has lived on minimum wage. His book royalties, which have become substantial, all go to the ministry, which in turn gives away large sums to missions organizations. Alcorn and his wife live in the same house they owned in 1990. Yet to his way of thinking, Alcorn says he has sacrificed nothing.

Others have, though. One of Alcorn's friends lost his house and his job and spent nine months in jail. That's part of the real-life penalty activists may pay when they practice civil disobedience.

Other activists take a less confrontational approach. On assignment for *Christianity Today* magazine I met women who lead crisis pregnancy centers all over the country. As a rule, they don't protest abortion. Their strategy is to give desperate women a real choice—a choice to have their baby if they want. CPCs provide pregnancy tests, counseling, support for pregnant women, medical care and post-abortion trauma counseling. These activists believe that few women want to have abortions, but they just don't know they have other options. CPCs provide care rather than confrontation and argument.

Then there is the political approach. Many activists reason that judges made abortion legal, and judges are appointed by politicians. If enough right-thinking politicians were in office, then right-thinking judges would follow. So these activists work for political campaigns, judging politicians more by their stand on abortion than by anything else.

★   ★   ★

There are many ways to work for justice, just as these examples show. No approach is perfect. Each approach tends to have its own unique momentum, sometimes leading to unexpected results. When activist movements are in start-up mode, you can't always see what the long-term implications will be.

That is where history comes in. We have a long, deep tradition of activism in America. I learned about it in preparing to write a series of historical novels on the American experience. I became convinced that the best way to step back and think about activism, to see the long-term implications of our choices, is to learn from history.

One activist who read this book in manuscript form was dismayed by its concentration on history. He wanted contemporary examples, not dead people. He found history inherently dull.

I don't. I am fascinated by the past, and I love to learn about it. But apart from personal taste, why focus so much on history?

I believe we gain certain advantages from history that we can gain nowhere else. First is a particular kind of encouragement. It helps to know that we are part of something much deeper than the contemporary scene. Women and men have shared our passion for justice through the generations. They have given their lives to shaking the system, and sometimes they have succeeded only after decades of dogged persistence. We cannot gain such a perspective by studying our contemporaries, because they are just as much in deep water as we are. Only history lets us see activism as a deep, honorable and effective tradition.

This book is like a collection of old family stories. It reveals the experiences of people like us who set out to change the world. They are our kind of people. Their stories help us to understand ourselves. They give us courage to be ourselves.

Second, history lets us learn from situations where we are not blinded by emotions or swayed by personal involvement. We can coolly assess what worked and what didn't when we look over issues of the past, because they simply aren't issues that make our blood run hot today.

Sometimes what look like the greatest triumphs turn out to be disasters. That was true of Prohibition. And sometimes unnoticed events turn out to have unbelievable impact. Who would have thought that a stay-at-home mother writing a melodramatic novel about the South would communicate more about the evils of slavery than a thousand passionate speakers at loud rallies? But that was certainly true of Harriet Beecher Stowe and her novel *Uncle Tom's Cabin*.

When you're in the middle of a movement, you have no idea how to tell the significant from the merely tumultuous. History helps us see what makes a lasting difference and what may turn out to be just a momentary excitement.

Last and perhaps most important, history teaches humility, a quality often in short supply in activist movements. When we walk and breathe with great activists of history, we see how hard it is to predict the future. The best-laid plans often go wrong. The most virtuous people end up causing unintended harm. There is so much in life we cannot know, so much we cannot predict, so much we cannot control. Wise men and women are deeply aware of this, and they are aware of their own potential for failure. Such humility does not stop them from action. It tempers them so they become strong, just as a knife is tempered by heat so its blade will stay sharp.

★ ★ ★

Today we particularly need lessons from history because we only recently emerged from a fifty-year period that obliterated a great deal of memory, especially among the many Americans who consider themselves activist Christians.

Through most of American history, Christians have been involved in trying to change the world. They considered it a natural expression of their faith. Three of the greatest American reform movements—abolition, Prohibition and civil rights—were directly and self-consciously led by evangelical Christians under evangelical principles. A fourth—woman suffrage—was not explicitly Christian, but Christians were heavily involved and often appealed to Christian principles. Nobody thought that strange.

Then between about 1930 and 1980, evangelical faith became separated from public affairs. Prohibition was the high-water mark of Christian influence in America, and as a result of its dramatic failure, many white evangelical Christians lost hope. Added to it were the discouraging fundamentalist-modernist controversy and the *Scopes* monkey trial. Most evangelicals withdrew from the public square. They let liberal Christians have the social gospel, while they adopted a Scofield Bible view of the world, in which the fiery destruction of planet earth and the miraculous removal of its Christians were the most prominent features of the future.

Evangelicals continued to help the needy, particularly if gospel preaching was part of the program. (Gospel missions offered meals and beds, always accompanied by an urgent offer of Jesus.) But politics and social reform they left to other people. (Some black evangelicals retained a very robust tradition of civic engagement, and that grew enormously through the civil rights movement. But there was little interchange between white and black.)

Then with amazing speed, expectations changed. Groups like the Moral Majority (started by pastor Jerry Falwell in 1979) and the Christian Coalition (founded in 1989) embraced politics from a conservative, evangelical perspective. Today most evangelical leaders consider it the Christian's duty to make a difference in the world. "If you don't like the way I'm fighting abortion, then tell me how you are fighting it," as one prominent leader put it when he was criticized for stridency.

By that time, though, almost all memory of involvement was lost. The very idea of Christians advocating for public causes created panic among secularists and dreams of utopia (a long-lost Christian America?) among true believers. The realism that comes from experience was missing. Nobody's parent or grandparent had been both evangelically minded and politically passionate. White evangelical Christians had lost the rich heritage of experience that might have guided them.

This book is meant to help retrieve some of that needed memory. What is it like to be an activist? How do faith and social reform affect each other? What are the problems, the dangers, the misconceptions, the struggles? Those who went before us can tell us, if we listen to their stories, so full of inspiration and admonition..

Chapter by chapter I will tell some of those stories, using their experiences to offer a kind of *Pilgrim's Progress* for activists: "This is the journey you are on. Here are the dangers to expect. This is the crucial signpost at which you must decide what path to follow."

I write this book for people who ache for the world and want it to change. They have not lost that first sense of surprise and dismay at discovering that life around them is not what it should be. They care. They want to do something. Poverty, injustice and suffering disturb them.

More particularly, I write for those who are beyond the first rush of idealism. Perhaps they began with a blast of enthusiasm. They favored simple generalizations and one-size-fits-all remedies. Experience has taught them, however, that the world does not have any ready-made handholds with which to flip it on its head. Change is difficult and sometimes brings unintended consequences.

There is great work to be done. Those who went before us have done their part with courage and fortitude. Their lives give encouragement—and warning. Now it is our turn. But we do well to pause and learn wisdom, because we are not the first to take this road.

STARTING WITH TRUTH

THE ABOLITION OF SLAVERY WAS THE first great reforming cause in American life. It arose like an unexpected storm out of the clear blue sky, for in the early nineteenth century slavery was very much an accepted part of American life. The American experiment had been going on for about fifty years, accompanied by a great flood of rhetoric about equality and freedom. Yet the horror of slavery had not irritated the public as much as a mosquito bite.

True, the Founding Fathers debated the compatibility of slavery with freedom. They saw the contradictions. But in the framing of the Constitution they made their peace with slavery, and within a generation that peace had become all-pervasive. In Washington, D.C., you could sit on the Capitol steps and watch black people drag their chains as they marched to the slave markets to be sold, their teeth to be examined like a horse's, their children to be offered as a separate packet to anyone with money to spend. You could watch a husband being torn from his wife as they were sold to separate buyers. None of the orators of liberty who held forth in Congress seemed to notice. Maybe it bothered their consciences, but they didn't say so. The country got exercised about British imperialism, about western lands or about the national banking system, but not about slavery.

The first question is, what got abolition going? What made people begin to care?

It is not easy to say. Antislavery seems to have begun randomly here and there all across the republic, through a chance conversation in one place, through an encounter with discrimination or slavery in another place, through an eccentric burst of individual conscience. Abolition did not start with any one great charismatic leader or with any one group of people in any one place. In England, antislavery advocates like William Wilberforce had been at work since 1791, but their cause seemed remote to most Americans. Abolition was not launched by a pathbreaking essay nor by a protest meeting. Efforts to explain abolition as the product of class interests have failed. Nor did antislavery have any natural political constituency.

Of course, some people had long been bothered by slavery. Many Quakers in particular opposed it. It would be wrong, however, to think of abolition as Quaker-inspired. Quakers kept to themselves, and their religion appeared strange to Presbyterians, Congregationalists, Baptists and Methodists. Such mainstream Christians were unwilling to take lessons from Quakers. At the inaugural meeting of the American Anti-Slavery Society, a third of the delegates were Quakers, but it was the last time that Quakers were so overrepresented. Ever after, antislavery meetings were dominated by those who had drunk from the well of evangelical Christianity. However, it would not be right to credit evangelical Christianity with launching the movement either. In fact, the vast majority of evangelicals remained untroubled by slavery.

So what launched American antislavery? Truth. A penetrating

truth broke through American lethargy, first with a few people here and there, eventually with larger numbers. The truth was simple: slavery is sin. Today the revelation that slavery is sin seems obvious, on a level with murder is sin. But at the time, it revolutionized the discussion.

Before then, discussions had centered not on *slavery* as an evil, but on *slaves* as an evil. Many saw slavery as posing a classic dilemma: we wish America had never had slaves in the first place, but now that they are here in great numbers and our economy depends on them, how do we get rid of them? People argued whether ignorant slaves were ready for liberty, and whether setting loose two million illiterate Africans would be dangerous to public safety and destructive to the national economy. Rights were also at issue—not the rights of slaves, but the rights of slaveholders. Surely their property was involved, and they would need to be compensated if their slaves were freed. Where would the money come from? The whole discussion was framed around such "practical" issues as security and economics. From a white man's point of view—and only white men had a voice—it was more prudent to leave things be.

Beginning in about 1830, thirty years before the Civil War, the truth that slavery is sin began to cut through this Gordian knot of practical worries. It simply would not allow, for example, a reasonable discussion of the vast expense of compensation to slaveholders for their lost property. Abolitionists asked, would you compensate thieves if they were caught and their stolen property restored to its proper owners? Neither would you compensate slaveholders for their lost slaves.

Abolitionists emphasized that slaveholding was essentially kidnapping. Maybe somebody else had brought the slave by force from Africa, but the slaveholder was an accessory to the crime because he knowingly and by force held captive a kidnapped human being. Even if the slave's grandfather was the one who had been kidnapped from the place of his birth, that hardly made it right to hold his grandson a captive.

The language of sin was well understood at that time. Christians knew that sin must lead to repentance, deep and from the heart. They knew that sinners prefer to talk about the logistics of reform because it offers excuses and delays. But sin is not a matter for practical discussion unless first the sinner has fallen on his knees and cried out, "What a wretch I am! What can I do to be saved?"

"Slavery is sin" dodged all the practical questions of how a slaveholding nation could transform itself into a non-slaveholding nation. By avoiding such questions and moralizing the discussion, "slavery is sin" infuriated slaveholders and their sympathizers. (Compare, for example, "abortion is murder.")

Even today I find that writing about slavery exposes the same divisions. Some readers will think me unfair for unapologetically offering the abolitionist point of view. They will point out that what seems sinful today did not appear so clearly sinful in 1830; that some slaveholders apparently *did* treat their slaves well; that the threat of violence and war was real, as Nat Turner's slave rebellion demonstrated; and that nothing in the Bible explicitly condemns slavery. All this is true, but it all serves to obscure the central problem: some men and women held the lives of other men and women without the slightest moral or legal justification. This was intolerable. This was sin.

To see slavery not as a problematic institution but as a sinful crime was the great truth that launched the antislavery movement. This truth created a movement for what was called *immediatism*.

Immediatism did not propose, as its opponents accused, that slavery must be ended in a day. It called on slaveholders and all who supported them to feel the horror of slavery and move to end it with the immediacy of someone who discovers a snake crawling up his or her leg. Immediatism was the equivalent of the sinner's question, "What can I do to be saved?"

★ ★ ★

Truth matters. This I learned from abolitionism. Even in a postmodern society where truth is relativized, truth has the power to move people. Absolute truth, true truth, core truth—truth that you believe in your gut, truth that you will bet your life on. Contemporary society prefers Pilate's question, "What is truth?" Even activists may grow fond of acting like hard-boiled skeptics. But the reality of unchanging truth cannot be undone by such skepticism. It exists at the core of human life. Such truth can launch a movement to change the world.

Somebody sees a homeless woman dressed in rags and says, "Nobody should live like that." That truth, so fundamental and beyond argument, has the potential to awaken the conscience not just of one person but of all that person's friends and relations. Skeptics may argue that it is very hard to help that homeless person. She is perhaps mentally ill, won't take her medicine and refuses help. So should we just shrug? Give her up as a hopeless case? "Nobody should live like that" is a truth that starts a fire in the belly of an activist who launches a movement to find a way to help.

Another person reads a newspaper story about persecuted Dalits in India and realizes, "Those are my sisters and brothers." In that truth lies the possibility of a movement to shake the caste system.

When abortion was first completely legalized by the Supreme Court's *Roe v. Wade* decision in 1973, many Protestants found the decision worrisome but few saw it as criminal. Most shrugged. Only a few recognized the fundamental truth that the fetus is a human life.

Wherever that truth was recognized, however, the terms of debate changed utterly. All concerns about the practical problems of an unwanted birth were dwarfed entirely by this: *that's a baby you want to kill.* With ultrasound movies of the baby in the womb, with amplified heartbeats, with photos of tiny hands and feet, the anti-abortion movement worked to spread that truth. Some were convinced by the evidence, and some were not. But wherever the anti-abortion movement has life and strength, it is because of that truth.

HIV/AIDS has a similar story. When the epidemic first struck America, it drew only lukewarm concern from most Americans. Many of those infected were homosexuals engaged in promiscuous sex and drug use. *They were asking for it,* many Americans thought to themselves, even if they were too polite to say so. Though the epidemic has spread to other groups, it remains true that many of those infected were "asking for it." They use drugs or practice unsafe sex.

The truth that changed the lukewarm response was simple: you don't turn your back on sick people. If somebody has lung cancer, you don't withhold treatment because he smoked. If someone is injured in a car accident, you don't ask how fast she was driving. You provide care, because caring for the sick is a fundamental commitment of a humane society. Care is automatic, or it should be. As that truth was remembered, people became ashamed of their first response.

★ ★ ★

Human beings are not naturally drawn to crusades. They are usually happy to go about their lives, making money, raising families and enjoying the world they live in. Yet, contrary to all that is natural, activist movements regularly occur. A select group of men and women become passionately involved in trying to change the world for others' benefit, not necessarily their own. They forsake comfortable lives, profitable careers and even happy families for campaigns that their own friends and relatives consider quixotic.

You could never engineer such sacrifice. Perhaps something in these activists' background predisposes them toward it, but they all have brothers and sisters raised under the same roof who manage to steer clear of it. If you ask the activists themselves, they will often say that some irresistible force grasped them. They felt that they had no choice but to respond. The force that invades their lives is truth. Fundamental truth gives an activist movement its power.

The truth may come to them like a searing flash of lightning, revealing a view so obvious and compelling that afterward they can talk of nothing else. So it happened to Martin Luther, when he understood that "the just shall live by faith." Or the truth may be something they discover that they have known from childhood but only recently understood in its full implications. Martin Luther King Jr. apparently had such a dawning revelation during his first year as a preacher in Montgomery, Alabama.

If you are attracted to an activist movement, you should ask yourself whether you can state, simply and powerfully, its core truth. That truth must sustain you for the long haul.

When I look back at the failings of my first activism against the Vietnam War, I sometimes think this was the problem. We had a sense that the war was wrong, but we could not articulate it simply and powerfully. Truthfully we were motivated more by fear of be-

ing drafted into the army than by truth itself. When the draft
stopped, so did the protests.

★   ★   ★

Truth is so powerful, so utterly life-changing for those who grasp
it, that they often believe it has power to do the work by itself.
They think that other people will respond just as they did. An activist's work is simply to preach the truth, they conclude, with an
appeal straight to the heart.

Spreading the truth, however, soon makes you recognize forces
that are obscuring the truth. Sometimes you find enemies among
people who seem, superficially, to be on your side.

That was so of the abolitionists, who found some of the greatest
enemies of the truth in the American Colonization Society, a strong
and respected movement that also sought to free slaves. Colonizationists were often leading citizens. They saw that slavery contra-
dicted American ideals and wanted to solve the problem in a way
Southerners could accept. Their proposal was to free slaves volun-
tarily and send them to Liberia in Africa. They sought either to
raise funds to buy slaves from willing sellers, or else to convince
slaveholders to donate their slaves to the cause. Nobody would be
forced to give up their slaves, they said; slavery would be gradually
and painlessly disassembled.

When abolitionists began preaching "slavery is sin," they soon
began to attack the colonizationists. How dare they pay the slaveholder for his crime? How dare they send slaves to a destination
they had not chosen? Even more devastatingly, abolitionists calculated that colonizationists had no reasonable prospect of freeing all
slaves. As a practical matter, colonization was equivalent to the plan

of a drunkard to quit drinking by cutting down one drop at a time.

William Lloyd Garrison led the way for abolitionists. His harsh assault on the American Colonization Society scandalized people. How could he speak in such a way to outstanding, well-meaning citizens? Garrison knew how to sting people, as his fellow abolitionists would soon learn. He stung colonizationists, and he stung slaveholders. They replied fiercely, attacking him as harshly as he attacked them.

Colonizationists thought that abolitionists should appreciate their reasonable, practical approach to slavery. They resented being preached at by people they considered fanatical and moralistic. But abolitionists saw that the apparent goodness of the Colonization Society, including its urbane, charitable attitudes, obscured the truth that slavery is sin. By obscuring the truth, in effect the colonizationists became the most dangerous defenders of slavery. They were allowing people to give a little money to the society to soothe their consciences.

The storm instigated by Garrison stirred others to write newspaper articles defending his position. In doing so, the writers discovered each other, a society of misfits sprinkled sparsely across the long stretches of the American countryside. As concerned individuals, they had hardly known that anybody else held such radical ideas. The controversy brought abolitionists to the surface. They began to form organizations to work together.

★ ★ ★

So it often happens today. Truth leads to conflict, and conflict sorts out friends and enemies.

If your conscience is awakened by the plight of the homeless, you soon discover that some people are dedicated to keeping things the same. A neighborhood association may oppose your attempt to open a homeless shelter because they worry it might drive property values down. Your commitment to spreading the truth that nobody should live like that will lead you to fight against the neighborhood association, shaming them for their values. You may find yourself alienated from former friends. In the process, though, you will discover your allies. The commotion and conflict will draw them into the open.

Personally, I find conflict hard to bear. I only want to do good; why should I have to fight anyone? But the truth has enemies. The history of abolition is a warning: if I stand for the truth, some people will stand against me. I had better be ready for that.

★   ★   ★

The founding meeting of the American Anti-Slavery Society took place in Philadelphia in December 1833, with just sixty people in attendance. They came fearful and intimidated by the threats of local thugs. Just months before, New York City abolitionists had started a local organization, and riots had erupted in the streets. America was a very racist* place, and it took a brave radical to publicly stand for African Americans and against slavery.

Those first abolitionists did not think of themselves as brave radicals. They were not accustomed to running from mobs. They called themselves Christians—mostly very orthodox, evangelical

---

*I find that some readers hate to hear America, or any group of Americans, described as racist. In our current scene, the race card is sometimes played in unfair ways to shut down discussion or anathematize a point of view. However, *racist* has an objective meaning, and that is how I use it. The vast majority of nineteenth-century Americans really believed Africans to be inferior, and they insisted that anyone with a drop of African blood be treated as inferior. They were not necessarily evil people in other respects, but they were certainly racist.

Christians. They chose to meet in Philadelphia, the city of brotherly love, hoping it would be more peaceful than New York.

The meeting's organizers approached Philadelphia civic leaders, asking them to preside over the meetings. But none of them was willing to attend, let alone to take a public stand against slavery. Abolition was simply too likely to inspire violent reactions. In the end, the abolitionists made do with Beriah Green, who headed the Oneida Institute, an upstart school in upstate New York. Disgusted by his fellow abolitionists' timidity, Green said, "If there is not timber amongst ourselves big enough to make a president of, let us get along without one, or go home and stay there until we have grown up to be men."

Green had been a professor at Western Reserve College, teaching religion in the wilderness of Ohio, when he came across some of William Lloyd Garrison's writings opposing colonization. Green grasped Garrison's logic and began to write against slavery in local newspapers. Vociferous local opposition pushed him to resign from the college and go to the newly formed Oneida Institute, a school where young men could work to pay for their education, and a place where reforming ideas were more readily accepted. At Oneida, Green fought to open the school to blacks, a move that would cause it to lose state support and ultimately to fail.

The convention delegates were a varied bunch. The dapper William Lloyd Garrison came from a different milieu than Green's: that of newspaper editors, printers and political gadflies. America was full of small, politically partisan newspapers. Garrison went from one to the next in the bitterly contested elections of the early nineteenth century. At one time he partnered with Benjamin Lundy, an idealistic Quaker editor who opposed slavery. During a sojourn in Baltimore with Lundy, Garrison met many African

American citizens and learned firsthand of their strong opposition
to going back to Africa as colonists. He began to see colonization
as an oppressive, anti-black scheme rather than as a benevolent
way to free blacks from slavery. Garrison returned to his native
New England and launched the influential antislavery newspaper
The Liberator.

Delegate Lewis Tappan came to the antislavery movement from
business. He and his brother Arthur ran the most successful dry-
goods store in New York City, wholesaling cloth to dealers
throughout the United States. The brothers were pious Presbyterians, New England–grown Calvinists, who lived simply and gave
away their substantial profits to all kinds of charitable causes. Between their money and their can-do organizational fire, the Tappan
brothers would help turn the abolition movement from a debating
society into an activist organization.

Samuel May was a Harvard-educated Unitarian pastor who
came from Boston to the Philadelphia convention—the only non-
orthodox believer in the founding group, unless you count the
Quakers. May was a warm, friendly, gregarious man who had the
courage of his convictions. When he met Garrison, everything fell
into place. He became militant in his antislavery convictions,
which cost him his church in 1836.

John Greenleaf Whittier, a Quaker, also came from Garrison's
circle. Unlike the energetic Garrison, Whittier was a moody, intro-
spective poet. Other notable Quakers who attended the convention were James and Lucretia Mott, wealthy merchants in the cot-
ton trade. Lucretia would later gain fame in the fight for women's
rights. She actually spoke up in the course of the Philadelphia de-
liberations—an unheard of thing in those days. But then, the abolitionists were unconventional in many ways. They even wel-

comed people of color to participate in the anti-slavery convention, including James McCrummell, a local barber and leader in the African American community.

They were all men and women of devout faith. Apart from that, they had little in common. They came from different regions. Some majored in religion and some in politics and some in business. Some were highly educated and some not; some were wealthy and some quite poor.

But their understanding that slavery is sin had created a great common bond. The meeting was sober and quiet, but it was filled with the emotional intensity of deep conviction. Even though they feared mob violence—which they would experience, and soon—they felt optimistic. They believed that people had only to hear and understand the truth, and they would be converted.

Those first abolitionists sincerely thought slavery would be undone without violence or coercion. Many of them expected America to change within a few years, at most. The truth would do it. How could the virtuous, religious, intelligent people of America resist such obvious truths?

Because of his writing talents, Garrison was asked to produce a statement of the aims of the new society. He labored all night on the product, and in the morning the delegates eagerly signed it. It is a revealing document.

Garrison's Declaration of Sentiments begins by describing the American Revolution and its Declaration of Independence, which had been signed at Philadelphia just fifty-eight years before. The American Anti-Slavery Society, Garrison wrote, would fight to bring the cause of liberty to its logical fulfillment:

We have met together for an enterprise without which that of our forefathers is incomplete; and which, for its magnitude, solemnity, and probable results upon the destiny of the world, as much transcends theirs, as moral truth does physical force. . . .

Their principles led them to wage war against their oppressors, and to spill blood like water, in order to be free. *Ours* forbid the doing of evil that good may come, and lead us to reject, and to entreat the oppressed to reject, the use of all carnal weapons for deliverance from bondage—relying solely upon those which are spiritual, and mighty through God to the pulling down of strongholds.

Their measures were physical resistance—the marshaling in arms—the hostile array—the mortal encounter. *Ours* shall be such only as the opposition of moral purity to moral corruption—the destruction of error by the potency of truth— the overthrow of prejudice by the power of love—and the abolition of slavery by the spirit of repentance.

Perhaps never in the history of activism has a more innocent statement been written. Someone might point out that abolitionists had no choice. They had to adopt a nonviolent, noncoercive approach because no other options were feasible. Their numbers and strength in relation to slavery were like a flea on the back of an elephant.

Subsequent actions showed, however, that they were completely sincere. They believed in the power of truth. They really did plan to bring down the great economic engine of slavery strictly through moral purity, truth and love. If slavery was sin, then liberation from it could only come when the sinners acknowledged their fault and repented. You cannot coerce repentance. You can only tell the truth. Abolitionists did that for the next thirty years.

★   ★   ★

Starting with truth and sticking to truth is crucial. Activists experience many frustrations. In facing those frustrations, they will undoubtedly have long discussions about tactics. And in thinking so much about tactics, they may be tempted to neglect the truth that got them started.

For example, advocates for the homeless often find themselves wrapped up in political discussions at the city-government level. Political intrigues can grow quite complex. Which factions support us? Which factions oppose us? The activists may get so wrapped up in political maneuvering, they lose sight of the truth that nobody should live like that. They stop talking about it. As a result, some of the moral clarity and energy goes out of their crusade. They begin to attract people who enjoy politics instead of attracting people who feel the fire of righteous concern for homeless people.

If you understand that activism springs out of truth, you must stick to truth.

3

MEETING RESISTANCE

BECAUSE THEY WERE MOTIVATED BY TRUTH, antislavery activists started out as great publishers and preachers of the truth about slavery. Almost the first thing the American Anti-Slavery Society did after leaving Philadelphia was to start a publishing crusade. Under Lewis Tappan's leadership, and with the Tappan brothers' money, they began to print newspapers, magazines and books, and to send them South. They published magazines for children, newspapers aimed at women and books for clergy—literally by the millions. They sent these to anybody they knew or had heard of in the Southern states. They virtually invented the idea of mass mailings.

They would have preferred preaching face-to-face, but it was dangerous to speak against slavery in the South. An abolitionist stood an excellent chance of being beaten, jailed or even killed. In Southern cities, rewards were posted for the delivery of certain abolitionists, "dead or alive." Arthur Tappan, in perhaps his only recorded attempt at humor, was supposed to have said this regarding the $100,000 offered for him: "If that sum is placed in a New York bank, I may possibly think of giving myself up."

The abolitionists reasoned that if they could not go south and take their message in person, they could send it in the form of printed materials. Underlying this practical motive was a deep conviction: truth was so powerful that printed words alone might bring slavery to an end.

As soon as Southern slaveholders understood that abolitionists were mailing literature into their homes and churches, they organized vigilante groups to invade post offices, seize whole sacks of mail and publicly burn it. What is more, President Andrew Jackson encouraged postmasters to censor abolitionist mail, calling it "unconstitutional and wicked."

Hearing that their publications were being confiscated and burned, abolitionists gradually realized that their postal crusade would not work. In its failure they saw how slavery kept a grip on the South, that Southerners would violate their own beloved Constitution just to keep from hearing the truth.

Abolitionists switched tactics and put increasing emphasis on sending out agents—traveling missionaries for the cause. Led by the smoldering, charismatic Theodore Weld, they trained "the Seventy," consciously named for the seventy disciples sent out by Jesus to go from town to town proclaiming the gospel. The abolitionist Seventy could not go south—that was too dangerous—so they went to small towns throughout the North, where they would stay ten or twelve days in one place. The North was no picnic either. The agents were usually forcibly opposed. Sometimes they were beaten, often shouted down. Many times they could get no building to meet in. They were always controversial, seen as rabble-rousers and troublemakers because they criticized slaveholders as sinners. Nevertheless townspeople would come out to hear them—there was very little alternative entertainment—and often they ended up convinced. At the end of ten or twelve days, a vote would be taken for or against an immediate end to slavery. The yeas almost always won. The antislavery agents would help organize a new antislavery society and then move on to the next town.

★ ★ ★

Much of the abolitionists' early strategy was shaped by the brilliant Theodore Weld. He was a man so concentrated and eccentric that some, on first meeting him, thought him insane. He dressed like a rough backwoodsman, and his long hair flew in all directions. He wore a dreamy, blank stare and often unconsciously hummed to himself during conversation. Yet on closer acquaintance, many considered him almost a god because of his tenderhearted concern for others, his intellect, his spellbinding verbal theatrics. As a student at Lane Seminary, Weld spearheaded the first public debate on slavery in 1834. That debate, carried out in the remote, far-western frontier of Cincinnati, would set a standard for abolitionists all over the country.

The debate took place just two months after the founding of the American Anti-Slavery Society, but it was a much bolder affair. Rather than huddling secretively as the Philadelphia abolitionists had done, not even daring to leave the meeting room for meals, the Lane students held public meetings just across the river from the slaveholding state of Kentucky. They were prepared to take on any opposition.

Cincinnati, though still a relatively small and remote city, was a key to the entire Mississippi watershed. With that fact very much in mind, Lane had been founded as a missionary outpost on a leafy hill just outside the town. In 1832 Boston's famous Lyman Beecher was persuaded to come head the school. Great things were expected for the cause of Christ.

But those great things did not include radical antislavery. That would have caused trouble almost anywhere, but it was particularly sure to do so in Cincinnati, so close to the South. Weld had chosen to attend the school for exactly that reason, however: it would have Southern students and a Southern audience. Weld wanted to try the case of slavery in public, as close to the opposition as he could get.

The faculty knew a debate on slavery would cause trouble, and they tried to dissuade the students from staging it. President Beecher did too. Respectfully, the students declined to take their advice.

They met for eighteen consecutive nights, two and a half hours per night. They expected a furious debate, but Weld had done such a good job talking individually to students that support for slavery had vanished. It turned out to be less a debate than a revival meeting. The students spoke for themselves, telling what they knew about slavery from firsthand experience. William Allan, from a prominent slaveholding family in Alabama, spoke at length on slavery's cruelty. A former slave, James Bradley, spoke for nearly two hours and brought the audience to tears.

After nine days, the students voted unanimously to favor immediatism, and after eighteen days, they nearly unanimously condemned colonization. They ascribed this astounding result to Weld's persuasiveness and great moral character. There was more to it than personality, however. Weld had a strategy for presenting truth, a strategy he had learned from his mentor, the great evangelist Charles Finney.

First, Weld stuck to principle, not sentiment. A lot could be said about the cruelty slaves suffered, but Weld put little emphasis on it. He put the stress on the slaves' human rights. As creatures made in the image of God, slaves had a right to choose their own life, to earn their own living, to follow God as they saw fit. Slaveholders argued that many slaves were better off than their free counterparts. Weld doubted it, but he chose to argue a more fundamental issue. He didn't want to produce pity for the slaves but rather moral conviction about slavery. To deny a person his or her *moral agency,* as they called the right to direct your own life, was a sin against God whether carried out with kindness or cruelty. If you kidnapped someone but fed him well in captivity, did that remove your complicity in kidnapping?

Second, Weld insisted on public debate. He wanted to talk to those who disagreed with him. When training the Seventy, Weld taught them to seek out the smartest, surest opponent available to challenge to a public debate. That would attract a better crowd and test the antislavery argument against its best opponents. Weld determined not to waste his time and energy on debates among abolitionists. In fact, he never attended the national meetings of the Anti-Slavery Society.

Third, the discussion should be thorough and deep. The eighteen days of debate at Lane were typical: Weld always sought to create a sense that every angle, every argument had been considered fairly and truthfully. That took time. When the Weld-trained agents went out to the small towns and villages of America, they spent a minimum of a week, and often two weeks, in earnest public debate each evening. The truth, abolitionists thought, did not lend itself to sound bites.

Fourth, they emphasized facts. Wherever possible, Weld brought in first-person testimony. Years later Weld would use this technique to write a highly influential book, *American Slavery As It Is.* The concept was simple and powerful. With the help of his wife, Angelina Grimke, and her sister Sarah—the two sisters had grown up in a prominent slaveholding family in South Carolina—Weld went through reams of old Southern newspapers, clipping short news reports, court filings and advertisements for slaves. The casual, one-line summaries—of whippings, dismemberments, killings and separations of families—might seem innocuous taken one at a time, but marshaled together by scores or hundreds, they made a terrible drumbeat. This testimony did not come from fevered slave sympathizers; it came from Southern newspapers. Nobody who read *American Slavery As It Is* could maintain the argument that slaveholding masters cared tenderly for their slaves.

The book would serve as raw material for Harriet Beecher Stowe's novel *Uncle Tom's Cabin,* which perhaps more than any single publication in the history of literature galvanized public opinion for a cause. During the Lane debate, Stowe had been a teenage girl living under the roof of her father, Lyman Beecher.

Fifth, Weld presented the truth to ordinary people, not the elites. At Lane his target was students, not faculty. As the leader of the Seventy, he focused on farmers and traders. He avoided cities in favor of small towns and villages, where the vast majority of ordinary Americans lived.

Finally, at the Lane debate Weld pressed for a decision. He was not content to simply stage a debate. Facts must lead to commitment. He trained the Seventy to lead the debates toward a vote in which each individual must declare himself. This was evangelical revivalism brought into the realm of activism. It had the advantage of treating truth seriously, not as something to be played with.

All six of these principles can be applied to activism in our own day. Activists should not only know the truth that undergirds their movement, they should think how to make it prominent. They should seek public discussion, searching for a good opponent to argue out the matter thoroughly and deeply. They should emphasize facts, even if it takes considerable research to learn them. They should carry on the argument for truth with ordinary people, not just with those in ivory towers. They should try to get people to commit once they have been given enough information to do so. Weld's principles make a solid foundation for an activist movement based on truth.

★ ★ ★

In the short term the Lane debates were a huge encouragement to an intimidated, fledgling antislavery movement. The near-unanimous result suggested that truth really would sway America, and quickly.

The longer-range result was muddier. Convinced that racial prejudice was a sin, the Lane students began to help blacks in nearby Cincinnati, particularly by starting schools so blacks could gain a rudimentary education. Such activism might have been forgiven had the students not insisted on mingling with blacks, too, even eating meals with them. Beecher told Weld, "If you want to teach colored schools, I can fill your pockets with money, but if you will visit in colored families, and walk with them in the streets, you will be overwhelmed."

The students would not back away from African American friendships, so ultimately they were expelled from the seminary. Most of them joined a fledgling institution that would become Oberlin College. Lane was never again the same.

★ ★ ★

The same muddy results plagued abolition nationwide. Initially the gospel of antislavery spread so fast that some abolitionists—Weld in particular—were confirmed in their belief that the whole North would be converted within a few years. As a result of the North's conversion, they supposed, family, church and business connections would go to work on Southerners. North and South were so closely connected that the gospel of antislavery would be translated north to south through personal interactions, which no censorship could stop.

Events did not turn out that way. In the North, momentum slowed after initial gains. The South grew more obdurate, more vociferous, more threatening as slaveholders saw the antislavery argument take hold. Soon it was impossible to discuss slavery in the South. Those who tried were driven out. Abolitionist James Birney, who would run for the presidency in 1840 and 1844, found it impossible to remain in Huntsville, Alabama, though he had lived there for years, serving as mayor of Huntsville and as a trustee of the University of Alabama.

Concerned that the slavery issue could destroy the Union, Congress refused even to receive petitions from antislavery groups. Eventually Congress would pass the Fugitive Slave Act, which required ordinary citizens to aid in the recapture of escaped slaves or else suffer the penalty of law. The act was part of the Compromise of 1850, an attempt to keep America from civil war. To abolitionists, it was a compromise with a bad conscience.

Garrison's Declaration of Sentiments depended on an optimistic reading of the American Revolution: that America was built on freedom and on the claim of the Declaration of Independence that "all men are created equal." Abolition would merely finish the work begun in 1776. But now experience showed that America was a compromise wrapped around a fib. There was no real commitment to freedom and equality. In fact, the economic and social forces that abolitionists called "the slave power" had their tentacles wrapped all around America.

True, antislavery sentiment eventually grew from a tiny splinter of opinion to a vague but deeply held majority opinion in the North. Northerners by and large grew unhappy with slavery, though most remained racists who by no means contemplated equality for blacks. But Northern unhappiness with slavery made no discernible impact. Fewer slaves were freed every year, and slaveholders grew increasingly resistant to change.

Some frustrated abolitionists lost faith in the movement and in God, drifting into passivity. "The great body of Abolitionists seem to be mere *passengers* on a pleasure sail," complained Theodore Weld to his friend Gerrit Smith in 1839, just five years after the Lane debate. Another friend, Charles Stuart, wrote to Weld in 1843, "The Anti Slavery heart of the nation wants re-rousing, and we can obtain no adequate means of re-rousing it. . . . So that I should despair were it not that 'The Lord reigns' and bids 'the Earth rejoice.'" It would not be long before Weld himself had given up abolition.

To say the least, abolitionists' naive expectation that simple truth would win a quick response proved badly mistaken. Naturally this disappointed them, most of all because of what it revealed about their fellow citizens. They saw a nation that was far from Christian. They found no "moral majority." The character of America was determinedly racist, they came to believe. Appeals to conscience were not only ignored, they were often violently resisted. This was true even in an era when the church grew rapidly and most Americans showed great respect for religion.

Long-time abolitionist Gerrit Smith expressed despair in 1855 when he concluded that "the movement to abolish American slavery is a failure." He saw this as a tragedy not only for slaves but also for all of America. "American slavery has left scarcely one sound spot in American character; and it is, confessedly, the ruler of America." He had lost all hope for moral change. "It is but too probable," he predicted, "that American slavery will have expired in blood before the men shall have arisen who are capable of bringing it to a voluntary termination."

★ ★ ★

From abolition I learned the first great paradox of activist movements. They begin with truth. Activists see something—they see it with unconditional clarity. Activists think that others will see the same reality and be compelled to act.

When activists tell the truth, however, they discover another truth that is far less palatable: most people do not want to hear. People will studiously ignore you, or if they cannot ignore you, they will try to silence you. The forces that work against change are strong and well defended.

Activism depends on truth. But truth does not necessarily succeed.

★ ★ ★

At about the same period that the antislavery movement was beginning another set of men and women began to see the damage done by alcohol abuse. Americans drank too much—a huge amount, by the standards of today. Then as now, the damage did not stop with the overindulging individual. Look at unemployment, poverty, family violence, rape, crime. You always find alcohol involved. In the early nineteenth century, new industrialism made reform even more urgent. A drunk farmer might make a mess of his plowing, but he could go home and sleep it off. A drunk factory worker, though, might lose his hand or even his life to a fast-whirling machine. Alcohol, which had always been destructive, had become dangerous in a whole new way.

The new temperance activists recognized a startling truth: that this familiar substance was evil and was destroying lives. And it was an extremely social evil, depending upon many people to produce the liquor, sell it and encourage its use in taverns and at social functions.

Temperance societies sprang up, often as associations of people who pledged not to drink or to get drunk, and who tried to convince their neighbors to join them. The American Temperance Society began in 1826, and the Washingtonian Total Abstinence Movement organized in 1840. The truth of alcohol's evil seemed plainly obvious to these activists. Surely the truth would be as obvious to others. Why would America choose to indulge in a poison?

They found, however, that while people could not refute their argument, they could laugh at it. They could resist by creating caricatures of temperance activists as prim and pious moralists. In fact, activists discovered, America was quite wed to alcohol, for it was unwilling to change or even listen seriously. Reform in alcohol abuse made fits and starts of seeming progress, even resulting in Maine's statewide prohibition law in 1851. In most places, though, these changes were stoutly resisted or undermined by corruption. Drunkenness carried on.

★   ★   ★

The movement for women's rights rose directly out of abolition-ism. Many women joined in the antislavery crusade, and because the cause was so unpopular and in need of workers, women were allowed to take active, public roles. Gradually women were trans-formed by the experience. They learned organizing skills. They got used to speaking up. After spending years asserting that black peo-ple deserved the fundamental right to direct their own lives, they began to think that surely women did as well.

In 1848 an ad hoc group of women met at Seneca Falls, New York. Just as Garrison had done in Philadelphia, they explicitly mimicked the Declaration of Independence: "We hold these truths to be self-evident: that all men and women are created equal." To advocates of women's rights, the argument was indeed self-evident. How could men treat their mothers and sisters as inferior?

Activists for woman suffrage campaigned for equal rights and found, to the bitterness of their souls, that America had no real commitment to equality. In fact, most Americans refused to see the suffering that women endured when their husbands abused them or deserted them. They would not consider the lives of women like Susan B. Anthony, consigned to powerlessness because they were not married. The woman's crusade would go on for generations without seeing significant progress. The truth did not set America's women free. Most remained the property of men.

★ ★ ★

When we get to civil rights in the 1950s, we encounter no naive optimism. Truth was at the core of the civil rights movement, but the African Americans who launched it had few illusions that their white neighbors would change just on being exposed to the truth.

Nevertheless, truth was revolutionary for those involved with the movement. They had known from childhood that black people deserved the same treatment as white people, but that truth had lain dormant under segregation. Now suddenly truth intoxicated them. They were free and they would act free.

In the beginning, in Montgomery, Alabama, civil rights activists like Martin Luther King Jr. hoped that some white Christians might join them in recognizing this truth. They hoped to find allies among white ministers and other committed believers, based on their shared understanding of the truth of the gospel. Unfortunately, their hopes for white Southern allies proved almost entirely vain, though some white people did come from the North to help. In the South, the more African Americans asked for barely decent treatment—a seat on the bus—the more they were reviled, threatened, jailed and beaten. Hardly any white Christians spoke up for them. The more blacks answered mistreatment with love and prayer, the more associations of white ministers met to take stands against them as a threat to the Southern way of life. Civil rights activists had known that they lived in a racist world, but they had not known how violently that world would fight to maintain its prideful sinfulness.

The truth, Jesus said, will set you free. Every activist experiences this freedom, and then, in the process of sharing the truth, also develops severe doubts about whether the truth is enough. If the truth is to set a society free, it is only through the crucible of suffering that develops when activists discover how deeply enslaved to sin their society has become. Freedom may come, but not without a cross.

★ ★ ★

The movement against abortion has followed the same pattern in our time. After *Roe v. Wade* in 1973, a small but growing number of people recognized that unborn children were being sacrificed by the millions, often for reasons very far from noble. Many of those unborn children were killed as a convenient form of birth control. The silent scream of those children became for antiabortion activists a truth they could not escape.

And yet antiabortion activists have learned that there is a fundamental unwillingness to hear the truth. Over the course of forty years they have gained a more jaded and skeptical attitude about their country and their neighbors. This learned cynicism has sometimes led to horrible, violent deeds, such as the killing of abortion doctors or the destruction of abortion clinics. More often it has contributed to the bitter divisiveness that has characterized American politics and religion. So it has often been when activists see a truth that does not set others free.

Pro-abortion-rights activists also began with truth: that women have a moral right to control their own bodies. Two truths come into conflict, and activists claim one and reject the other. The result may be far from ennobling.

★   ★   ★

These stories about truth offer a double-sided message. On one hand, they remind us that truth is the basis for activism. I have often seen frustrated activists take what they consider a more practical approach that leaves truth behind. For example, they may choose tactics of protest and civil disobedience, reveling in the publicity and fervor they can generate. They may find that emotional appeals or simplistic sound bites produce more support than carefully reasoned appeals to truth. They may put their energy into promoting celebrity protestors rather than engaging in serious dialogue or debate. They may even flirt with threats and violence.

As I look around at the contemporary scene, I see the attraction of all those approaches. Sometimes truth seems too slow. To leave truth behind, though, or put it far in the background, is to lose touch with the mainspring of the movement. Without a firm and constant reference to truth, activists eventually lose energy or fly off in an unguided direction. Movements need to willingly engage the arguments against them, to seek out public debate and engage in it with depth and thoughtfulness. Protests and sound bites have a purpose in activist movements, and so do tactical discussions. But they should not be allowed to substitute for the presentation of truth.

The second side of the message is equally important: truth, no matter how carefully and thoughtfully presented, will not necessarily be heard. Activists need to consider what theologians call the fallenness of humanity.

Perhaps you started out thinking people are basically good-hearted. You found it easy to get along with others, and you took their cordiality at face value. Then you became an activist, and you discovered a darker side to your neighbors' character. They don't want to hear about it. When you talk about the truth, you find a stubborn, hard-shelled indifference under their genial surface.

The activist who experiences such resistance often ends up angry at society. With such feelings comes a great temptation to self-righteousness and impatience toward those outside the activist movement. I have seen too many activists who are fundamentally hostile, lacking humility about their own failings and ready to instantly convict people who don't see things the way they do. The reaction is understandable but not helpful.

Human beings do not necessarily do what they know to be right. They will act from their own selfish interests and justify themselves in their most willful and sinful behavior. They will sometimes do pure destruction, even to themselves. The pathway that leads from truth to virtuous living must pass through the human heart, and there it can be twisted and skewed.

This means that activists may have to persist for a long time. It means they may have to suffer before the truth wins out. And so I have to ask myself: is the truth I have come to believe worth a lifetime?

Activists need grace, to forgive the sinners who refuse to pay heed to the truth. They need love, to persist in doing good and in presenting the truth despite being rebuffed. Human lives will not be changed by truth alone, but by love and grace. It takes such virtues to persist in spite of rejection.

Essentially this is the Christian story: the God who seeks to change the world is willing to persist. He persisted for centuries, and he even suffered himself in order to win over humanity that prefers to suppress the truth. This God is the model for activists. He was the model for Martin Luther King Jr., who refused to hate and who was willing to suffer and die because he believed in the transformation truth could bring.

I don't mean, of course, that activists must all be Christians like King. Activists come from all kinds of religious traditions, or from none. But the Christian story, which is all about change, provides an essential template for those who want to change the world. Fundamental is the belief that truth can set people free. Equally, the Christian story presents truth as needing the power of love— love that persists even with those who refuse to hear.

4

PRESSURE TACTICS

THE TERM "INSTITUTIONAL SIN" IS CONFUSING, I think. People, not institutions or systems, are sinners. An institution does nothing good or bad except at the bidding of people.

Nevertheless, institutions play a large part in shaping the way we sin—and in keeping us from breaking free. A spider's web of institutions, laws, habits and customs make a flexible, tough network that holds sinners tight and reinforces their will to resist change. To cite just one example, a shoe manufacturer may believe that the low wages he pays Asian employees are unfair, but he knows (or believes, anyway) that competition forces him to pay the same low wages others pay. He feels powerless to change his behavior because of the economic system.

So activists discover, often with dismay, that they must attack this whole web that binds people to injustice. It is not enough to simply present truth and change people's hearts, one by one. Activists must change laws, institutions, habits and customs, for these bind people's dark hearts together into a formidable fortress. Activists must shake the system.

★   ★   ★

Abolitionists developed a term for the systemic nature of slavery: "the slave power." They had set out to convince slaveholders to repent of their sin and to free their slaves, but they discovered that the problem of slavery was larger than the individual sins of slaveholders. It was bound up in a Southern economy built on slave labor. Northern traders, bankers and industrialists contributed to this slave economy even though they might never see a slave, let alone own one. Slavery was also the foundation of the Southern social system, in which people gained status from their relation to the Southern nobility—all slave masters. It extended into Congress, where politicians dedicated themselves to an aggressive defense of slavery and made it impossible for the main political parties to even discuss slavery. It found its voice in churches that indignantly refused to contemplate criticisms of slaveholders, some of whom were ministers and bishops, and bolstered the defense of slavery with biblical arguments. Slavery was built into the mores and customs of society at every level, North and South.

The slave power had no conscience that activists could appeal to. It was a ten-headed organism that operated by its own blind instinct. Furthermore, as abolition grew, the slave power responded by becoming more aggressive, more threatening and more expansionist. It drew the whole country into its web.

In 1854 federal troops lined the streets from the courthouse to the wharf in a major U.S. city. Through furious crowds of protestors, Anthony Burns, an escaped and recaptured slave, was forcibly escorted by federal soldiers onto a federal ship, back to a life of slavery. Was this some Southern city, dedicated to slavery? No. It was Boston, the virtual capital of abolition. Few people in Boston supported slavery, but the law was the law. Despite a frenzy of defiant oratory and violent attempts to storm the courthouse and free

Burns, during which one man was killed, the government kept solidarity with the slave power. Did Massachusetts government officials do this because they actually believed in slavery? No, but they thought the orderliness of society depended on upholding the law.

Abolitionists needed to dismantle the slave power—which they had no idea how to do. In the end, only the carnage of the Civil War accomplished it.

★ ★ ★

Move forward one hundred years, and you find segregation as the new "slave power." Though many people, north and south, believed segregation to be immoral, it survived almost unchallenged because of a web of legal and cultural forces.

In 1954 the city of Montgomery, Alabama, was a modest, shaded, old-fashioned Southern town, leaning on its past. As state capital, it harbored ideas of genteel Southern living. (Birmingham, by contrast, was a rough-edged, industrial maelstrom of steam and steel, known for its mean heart.) Montgomery was sunk in the stasis that goes by the name of tradition. Tradition meant segregation.

Nobody expected anything new to happen in Montgomery, but it was there of all places that the civil rights movement first found its stride. It was there that Rosa Parks refused to give up her seat to a white bus rider and was arrested and thrown in jail.

It had long been a sore point that some Montgomery bus drivers went out of their way to treat African Americans, their best customers, disrespectfully. Yet numerous complaints with the bus company and the city authorities had failed to register. These authorities knew, certainly, that disrespectful treatment was ignoble. Their deeper loyalty, however, was pledged to segregation. So when complaints came against the segregated seating arrangement on buses, which seemed calculated to rub in black inferiority, the authorities treated the arrangement as though it had come down from Mount Sinai with Moses. Remember the spider web? Segregated seating was senseless and mean, but it was one strand of that web.

For years the local chapter of the NAACP had looked for a case to legally challenge these seating arrangements, which required black people to sit in the back and to surrender their seats to any white person. Rosa Parks's arrest seemed tailor-made for such a legal test.

Parks made the perfect picture for the cause. This slightly husky, spectacled figure of respectable Negro rectitude was a church woman who worked hard at her menial job altering garments at a department store. She had quiet dignity; she was not much of a talker, but she could express herself intelligently when she needed to. Such a woman surely deserved polite treatment. Instead, she was treated rudely and violently.

Within hours of Parks's arrest, word of the scandal spread through the African American neighborhoods. For such a woman to be ordered to give up her seat after a long day of work, to be arrested, handcuffed and jailed for refusing, was the outer limit of the utter frustration of segregation. You could never be good enough. You could never earn respect. You were always a second-class citizen. If Rosa Parks could be treated like that, what hope for the rest of us?

A boycott was organized against the bus company. This was not an appeal to the truth of human dignity. It was meant to slap back. If the bus company could not treat blacks decently, they could do without the blacks' money. The boycott was a tactic designed to get the bus company's attention, to show its officials that they could be hurt too.

★ ★ ★

A boycott is a pressure tactic, designed to make people uncomfortable, designed to shake the system. Strikes and protests are also pressure tactics. They rarely make a moral appeal or advance a discussion about the truth. As often as not, they stop reasonable discussion because they make people angry. When César Chávez called a boycott against California table grapes, he was not trying to appeal to the conscience of California farmers on behalf of their mistreated workers. He was trying to force them to negotiate by threatening their livelihood. He was trying to shake the system.

Pressure tactics make many people uncomfortable, because they have more to do with power than with truth. We understand a personal, heartfelt challenge, one-on-one, but pressure tactics seem to be impersonal, blunt instruments.

But what were the plagues of Egypt, if not a pressure tactic? Why did Jesus tear up the temple courts, if not to force people to pay attention? The struggle against injustice and sin involves confrontation. It involves shaking the system so that people can get free of its web.

I recently listened to Mary Nelson talk about her work with Bethel New Life on Chicago's West Side. Bethel New Life has grown from a small beginning twenty-seven years ago—an aging Lutheran church deciding to rehab a three-flat apartment building in a decaying neighborhood—to an organization with 348 employees involved in everything from banking to transportation. Bethel New Life claims to have built more than one thousand housing units in their neighborhood. They have made a difference in their community.

Nelson emphasizes how important it is to work with and sometimes pressure politicians, government agencies and banks. She described an effort to get a local bank to sign off on a loan program that would make it possible to expand low-income housing. The bank president stonewalled them, so they organized a rally on the steps of his bank. Having invited prominent local politicians, they turned those politicians' interest in votes into pressure on the bank president. Then they pursued the bank president into his own elevator. By chance, the elevator got stuck between floors. In the small confines of the elevator, the activists badgered the bank president. Finally he agreed to sign the papers that made the government loans possible.

He never lost a dollar on the loans, but it took pressure to make him see that signing was the right thing to do. As bank president, he did only what was customary—and that didn't include loaning money to poor people. He didn't want to change his approach to banking. Pressure tactics got him to think again.

★   ★   ★

Pressure tactics do not always work, though, and they rarely proceed smoothly or easily. So it was in Montgomery, Alabama.

Rosa Parks's complaint about segregated seating got caught up in the soaring rhetoric of a new preacher in town, a young Baptist intellectual with the inspiring name of Martin Luther King Jr. It happened almost by accident. Up until that time, King had shown little interest in any social cause, and certainly not in the bus system. Members of his church were of the class that was pleased to say they didn't have to ride the bus. They could afford to drive.

King recognized the passions generated by Rosa Parks's arrest, however, and before he quite knew it, he was leading a movement.

"We, the disinherited of this land," he preached in his first soaring address at the Holt Street Baptist Church, "we who have been oppressed so long, are tired of going through the long night of captivity." In that first ecstatic protest meeting, he told the jam-packed crowd of worshipers that "if we are wrong—God Almighty is wrong!" The crowd "seemed to explode," according to Taylor Branch's account in *Parting the Waters.* "If we are wrong—Jesus of Nazareth was merely a utopian dreamer and never came down to earth! If we are wrong—justice is a lie! And we are determined here in Montgomery—to work and fight until justice runs down like water, and righteousness like a mighty stream."

In case anyone was in doubt, King made clear that the struggle was about much more than a seat on the bus. It was even more than a matter of decency and dignity. He set the cause next to the integrity of God Almighty and Jesus Christ.

Juxtaposed to that mighty oratory, however, the demands that King and other leaders put to the city sound paltry. Here is the complete list of what they asked for:

1 Courteous treatment by bus drivers.

2. Seating of Negro passengers from rear to front of bus, and white passengers from front to rear, on a first-come-first-served basis with no seats reserved for any race.

3. Employment of Negro bus operators in predominantly Negro residential sections.

What particularly jumps out is the first request: "courteous treatment." That speaks volumes about the toxic nature of segregation and its impact on the lives of those afflicted by it. For African Americans, it was wearisome to an extreme, to live in constant interaction with people who treated you so shabbily and held all the power. Segregationists might defend their laws, but they could never justify their mistreatment of fellow human beings, their basic unkindness. All the legal injustices flowed from that sin of disregarding others.

Worse things were done, of course, than denying a middle-aged woman a seat on the bus. But Rosa Parks's mistreatment was so pointless, so demeaning. At its heart, the Montgomery bus boycott was not a legal challenge or an economic challenge. It was a moral challenge. And the moral challenge was this: why can't you treat a fellow human being with decency? The bus boycott put an exclamation mark on that question. It was designed to pressure Montgomery citizens so that they would hear the truth and respond.

★   ★   ★

Some white citizens of Montgomery wanted to answer that complaint. Letters to the editor of the local paper were at first mainly sympathetic to the boycotters' cause. Juliette Morgan, the reclusive city librarian from a well-known family, wrote to the *Montgomery Advertiser* in admiration for the boycotters: their "willingness to suffer for great Christian and democratic principles should inspire deep admiration among decent whites." Another woman wrote, "I have yet to find one person who feels that it is right that a Negro be made to stand that a white person may sit."

But very soon segregation's web of institutionalized and customary sin took hold and silenced those expressions of conscience. Morgan was harassed—stones thrown through her windows, tricks played on her at the library, insults offered on the street. She was a sensitive soul, and this response shattered her. Isolated and shunned by white society, she ultimately took poison and killed herself.

Montgomery's city fathers responded to the boycott with a show of toughness—canceling bus lines in black districts, arresting cab drivers who offered rides at a reduced fare to boycotters, and working behind the scenes to divide the city's black leadership. King was arrested and thrown in jail. A bomb was thrown at his house. A grand jury began handing out indictments against boycott leaders for violating state law. "We are committed to segregation by custom and by law," the report read, "and we intend to maintain it."

Black people were dismissed from their jobs, fined or held on bail for made-up charges. Once arrested and fined, the boycotters had to depend on able lawyers to take their cases to appellate courts. The leaders of the boycott spent more and more of their time either strategizing their legal cases or traveling the country raising money to pay the legal bills. Month after month, the boycott dragged on. Black people grew tired of walking to work. It was hard to sustain energy and hope, and the movement lurched from one crisis to another.

They never did get the white community's attention. After a year of the protests, the U.S. Supreme Court delivered a decision (*Browder* v. *Gayle*) that the bus company's segregated seating was illegal. Relief and euphoria washed over Montgomery's black population. They could hardly believe that unknown, insignificant black people in Montgomery, Alabama, who could not even get the officials of a local bus company to listen to them, had reached all the way to the Supreme Court of the most powerful nation on earth. Their cause had been vindicated, their patience and hard work rewarded. Of course they were inspired.

Ever after, students of the civil rights movement would wish they had been in the Holt Street Baptist Church on that first night, and on many nights thereafter in the other black churches of the city, to participate in the soul-stirring singing, praying and preaching. Images of Montgomery endure: poor black people walking in all weather to earn the simple dignity of a seat on the bus. Harder, more bitter times would come, but they did not stain the Christian nonviolence of the Montgomery bus boycott.

In that light, the campaign sometimes seems to tell a story of truth triumphant. Yet in fact, Montgomery did not achieve what people had hoped for: a moral victory. It did not even achieve its tactical aim, to get the white community to listen to its complaint. Black people came away invigorated, hopeful and inspired. Not so the white people. Nobody in the white power structure apologized for the hurt and abuse they had inflicted on black people. The white community actually became more hardened in its self-righteousness. Legally integrated buses were shot at, and city fathers bitterly threatened to shut down all bus service. Bombs were planted in African American homes and churches. In a few short years, Alabama would elect as governor George Wallace, who had made his reputation as a hard-nosed, unyielding segregationist. If you leave the Supreme Court and Northern opinion out of it, Montgomery was a failure.

This is the dissatisfying possibility when you use pressure tactics. The system often fights back, and then all you achieve is a fight. Even if you are victorious in pressuring institutions and systems, the results are likely to be partial, political and not particularly moral. Grudging compromises are the most probable endpoint. Activists may end up tired and disappointed, even when they win. It is not unusual for them to quarrel among themselves. In Montgomery the victors sniped at each other over whose home had been bombed most often, as though that were a prize.

It would take years of painful protests, voter registration drives, beatings and murders, to say nothing of legal and legislative drudgery, to break segregation's hold. Strand by strand, the spider's web of segregation law was torn, mostly because federal law superseded it. Once blacks could vote, could go to integrated schools, could enter any public establishment, segregation's control over an individual's moral actions dwindled. The web broke. Positive spaces grew. Respectful relationships became possible.

★　★　★

When I was a boy, I worked in an almond orchard near my home. To harvest almonds in those days, we spread tarps under the tree and then shook the almonds out. But it wasn't as simple as it sounds. You could hit and shake the tree with all your strength and get hardly any almonds to fall. But we also had a tool, a heavy ball of rubber attached to a stick. For some reason, if you hit the tree with that rubber ball, it would vibrate the tree just right and the almonds would cascade down.

That is the power of pressure tactics. The wrong approach will take all your energy and yield negligible results. The right one will vibrate the tree just right, leading to a cascade of result.

The system will resist change; pressure tactics can shake people loose from the system. If you want to change the world, you have to figure out how the system works and then how to shake it. Sincerity and moral conviction are not enough. Tactics really do matter.

Even when you find just the right tactics, however, a lot can go wrong. After you shake the almonds from the tree, you still have to pick them up. People who want to change the world are often ill equipped to accept the partial, practical results gained through pressure tactics. They may even disparage modest, tangible, negotiated gains. Patience, persistence and pragmatism may seem like weaknesses to them, rather than necessary strengths.

What may attract them is the excitement and publicity that pressure tactics produce. They like knocking the almonds down. They can mistake the sizzle of confrontation for genuine achievement.

When Mary Nelson was done harassing the bank president into signing for loans, she needed to make him a partner in economic development. Passionate activists might like to cast him as an eternal enemy. They might like to continually raise the stakes in fighting against the bank. But such an approach will likely undermine their own victories.

After Montgomery, the civil rights movement struggled with how to carry on in the wake of victory. Martin Luther King Jr. joined with other black preachers to form the Southern Christian Leadership Conference (SCLC), headquartered in Atlanta. Ella Baker ran the office and crafted detailed plans for grass-roots organization and voter registration. These were local activities designed to make a local difference in the segregated South. But the big-time preachers who dominated leadership in the SCLC could not focus on something so small and small-town: they wanted smashing visibility. They wanted another Montgomery.

They tried for a dramatic triumph in Albany, Georgia, marching and going to jail in vast numbers to desegregate the community. They failed, and in the process all but wrecked a vital local movement. They tried for a dramatic triumph in Birmingham and succeeded, putting segregation on trial on the national nightly news. Dogs and fire hoses attacked child marchers. Thousands were arrested and jailed while a fascinated nation watched on TV. But television viewers never learned that the triumphs of Birmingham had begun with a local organization led by the Reverend Fred Shuttles-

worth, a fearless bantamweight Baptist who had built a local movement willing to confront the meanest police force in the state.
Shuttlesworth got pushed into the background when the other
SCLC leaders came to town; and once the SCLC left town, Birmingham returned to its former self. The SCLC had used the city
for a national stage and used pressure tactics to gain national attention. But they left Birmingham itself little changed.

Sometimes pressure tactics fail—often spectacularly, since they
are so public and brash. Sometimes pressure tactics succeed, shaking the system and breaking open new possibilities. Nearly always,
though, they require something more. Pressure tactics are only
step one. They must be followed by a positive, practical program,
often marked by negotiation, compromise and reconciliation at the
local level.

★ ★ ★

A younger civil rights group grew up in the shadow of the SCLC,
the Student Nonviolent Coordinating Committee (SNCC). Like
the SCLC, it was built on strong personalities, but to a far greater
degree it was fueled by a risk-everything youthful recklessness.
The organization burst into existence during the rash of lunch-
counter sit-ins in 1960. Beginning as an ad hoc emergency coordinating committee for student leaders, it grew into an organization
with a mind of its own.

King and the SCLC welcomed the SNCC students' energetic
participation, but there was a vast difference between the preachers with their refined political pecking order and the poverty-
stricken, nothing-to-lose students. Ella Baker grew tired of the
preachers and went over to the students; they absorbed her practi-

cal, grass-roots approach, which suited their talents. SNCC used pressure tactics: demonstrations and protests. But their main approach involved convincing local blacks to register to vote, in spite of fear and intimidation. SNCC believed that whites could not continue to repress blacks if the black community in the rural South gained the courage to stand up for itself. They tried to build up the internal strength and cohesiveness of Southern black communities. It was a form of what came to be called community development, another way to shake the system by developing an alternative center of power.

The climax of SNCC's work was the Mississippi Freedom Summer of 1964. SNCC took on Mississippi as the heart of darkness, a place of poverty, ignorance and violent repression. Votes were key to fundamental change, they thought, and so they embarked on a crusade to register poor black people to vote, in defiance of threats and violence and even murder. To shake the system, SNCC invited hundreds of idealistic white students from the North, many who had no experience in the South. It took tremendous courage for them to come, and tremendous courage for SNCC to take them on. On the first day of the project, three SNCC volunteers turned up missing. Their bodies were eventually found buried in a rural dam. Student volunteers spent the rest of the summer watching every car that followed them on narrow rural roads and listening at night to every rustle of grass in the gardens outside their bedrooms.

Freedom Summer offered little fodder for the TV cameras. It required quiet meetings with black sharecroppers frightened of doing anything to draw attention to themselves. It meant conducting Freedom Schools to teach rudimentary literacy and history so that registration barriers could be breached. It meant organizing the Mississippi Freedom Democrats as an alternative to the all-white

Democratic political party. Most of this work was done in stifling summer heat, in parties of two or three sitting and sweating on front porches. It was tedious work, two steps forward and one back. Fear of the Ku Klux Klan dogged it.

SNCC gained considerable success that summer, but in the end it was easier to focus on the failures: the fact that the Mississippi Freedom Democrats were not fully recognized at the nominating convention of the Democratic Party in Los Angeles, that most Mississippi blacks did not register to vote and that relationships with young, idealistic whites who participated in the project grew very tense.

SNCC lacked the spiritual strength to deal with these difficulties and disappointments. Though most of its members came out of the black church, the high-octane urgency of their campaign pulled them away from the more sedate and conservative rhythms of church life. Many followed chaotic schedules. Immorality was common. They had few adult mentors and very little day-to-day discipline. They simply responded to crises.

This made a poor foundation for the patience that community development requires. After that Freedom Summer, SNCC abandoned most grass-roots efforts and adopted an increasingly apocalyptic, messianic approach. Instead of trying to register Mississippi blacks to vote, they set their goal as the eradication of racism in America. Rather than looking for allies to build organizations in Georgia, they looked for alignments with revolutionary movements in Africa and the Caribbean. As Charles Marsh writes, "SNCC went cosmic." The organization resolved to become a "Third World Coalition of revolutionaries who were anti-capitalist, anti-imperialist, and antiracist." A grandiose sense of SNCC's importance grew. "We are, without a doubt, vocally the most militant organization in the Civil Rights Movement," they proclaimed.

SNCC had always attracted good talkers—activist movements do—and now these good talkers talked themselves out of a job. It was perhaps a kind of self-soothing tactic, to rant against racist America, to promote black consciousness, to decry global systems, rather than to continue working for goals that could be measured, that would have immediate and practical effects on the lives of black people. Marsh refers to SNCC's choice as revolutionary Gnosticism because of its tendency to speak in terms of metaphysical good and evil, with evil being fought at the level of abstraction rather than of flesh and blood.

We see a lot of the same approach today, with legions of protestors eager to protest global capitalism, environmental degradation and world poverty, but often at the level of abstract principle rather than in a way that offers an actual poor person any practical help. Abstractions are necessary, but they must go on to making a practical difference. Otherwise they become just hot air. Combating systemic sin seems always to raise temptations of grandiosity.

★   ★   ★

Pressure tactics enabled the civil rights movement to grab the attention of white Northern America, and so ultimately to dismantle the legal side of segregation. Eventually that led to the whole system's collapse. The debris left behind after that collapse—the inequities, racism, rage—called for a second phase of the civil rights movement, but the movement lost its effectiveness at that more personal and local level. SNCC's program of community development could have helped, but it required more patience and maturity than its members possessed.

Pressure tactics run their course. They often function like fireworks: they make a lot of noise and gain attention in bursts. Then the real work begins—unless people mistake the fireworks for the genuine transformation.

For all the problems that come with pressure tactics, they have the potential of shaking the system. They did dismantle segregation, an achievement that seemed as remote as the planet Jupiter in 1955 when Rosa Parks was arrested.

Likewise, after years of frustrated activism, pressure tactics finally got women the vote.

★　★　★

Today the truth seems obvious that women are citizens and deserve a full voice in our democracy. It seemed equally obvious to woman suffrage activists in the nineteenth century.

Who opposed them? The only groups that consistently fought against women's rights were the brewers and distillers, because they believed women would use the vote to restrict alcohol sales. (It was no accident that when women finally got the vote, Prohibition went into effect in the same year.) Otherwise, opposition to woman suffrage was disorganized almost to the vanishing point. Women were more ignored and patronized than opposed.

If women held a meeting, it might prompt a newspaper editorial explaining that women were like a flowering vine that needed the strength of a (male) tree to hold it up. Or the wise guys at the saloon might wonder aloud why women wanted the vote when they already controlled their husband's. But the women were allowed to hold their meeting, pass their resolutions, write to the newspaper, visit their congressmen. Nobody bothered them, as a rule.

Yet year followed year, and women still could not vote. They did not even get close to the ballot box. It was like fighting a gigantic sumo wrestler whose greatest strength was his immobility. Opposition came indirectly, through custom and habit, from traditional attitudes and expectations. Even the majority of women were disinterested. It took the women's movement seventy years of hard struggle and argument to overcome this systemic, culture-laden resistance to change.

The two most famous women of the woman suffrage movement are, deservedly, Elizabeth Cady Stanton and Susan B. Anthony. They pioneered the movement beginning in about 1848 and persevered until their deaths early in the twentieth century. Stanton and Anthony never succeeded, however. Carrie Catt and Alice Paul are far less honored, but they are the leaders who actually got the vote for women. After years of fruitless effort, they led the women's movement in triumph, and they did it through pressure tactics.

The two women accomplished the goal together, but from opposite sides of the street. Carrie Catt was a formidable woman. Tidy, middle-aged, intelligent, perfectly turned out, unflappable and determined, she ran the National American Woman Suffrage Association (NAWSA). It was the established organization, with a long history of conventions and speeches. Picture well-to-do ladies in elaborate hats and you have a rough idea. Then in 1915, Catt took the helm and, like a Napoleon, organized the troops. She developed a detailed secret strategy that every state organization was required to sign off on. The plan called for complete submission of the state organizations to the national executive, and it insisted on leadership that worked full-time rather than fitting the work into free time between personal and family concerns. Catt's plan was essentially political, to lobby, cajole and campaign at every level of government. The plan was secret because she did not want the opposition—the brewers and distillers—to know where to oppose them. The women thought they could generate more passion in more places than their profit-motivated opponents could. They planned to make so much commotion and nuisance that it would be impossible to ignore them. Today the grassroots lobbying done by the National Rifle Association or by Focus on the Family is little different.

Alice Paul was from an entirely different generation than Catt. She was younger, slimmer and much more radical. She led the National Woman's Party, which had split off from NAWSA in 1914. The world was in the midst of World War I when Paul's group began to picket the White House, something no respectable group had ever done. Today picketers regularly carry outrageous signs in front of the White House, so it is hard to imagine how upsetting people found the tactic. President Woodrow Wilson, whom Catt had worked hard to befriend, was deeply offended, especially by signs the women carried claiming that the United States could hardly fight for democracy since it was not a democracy—half its citizens were denied the vote.

The women were attacked by onlookers, with the police standing by. They were knocked down, dragged away from the White House, their signs destroyed. Later the District of Columbia police began arresting them and taking them to jail. When brief jail sentences did not stop their protests, longer prison sentences were given—as much as six months for the crime of obstructing the sidewalk. (The men who daily attacked these women were never arrested or charged.) Claiming that they were mistreated in prison, the women went on hunger strikes. They were then force-fed.

Catt and NAWSA did everything possible to separate themselves from Paul's tactics, which they saw as hysterical and unproductive, not to say unpatriotic in the face of war. But unquestionably, the National Woman's Party forced the question of woman suffrage on the politicians, removing it completely from the realm of tea parties and women's clubs. It seemed there would be daily chaos in front of the White House until the women got their way. The confrontation preoccupied the newspapers, with Wilson and his administration coming off badly.

There is plenty of room for debate as to whether Catt's or Paul's approach had the greatest impact. They illustrate two different kinds of pressure tactics. Catt and NAWSA functioned within the American political system, suggesting by their respectful behavior that if women got the vote, they would behave reasonably and responsibly. Paul and the National Woman's Party, on the other hand, were deliberately disrespectful. Their tactics suggested there would be no peace or reason *until* women got the vote. Inadvertently the two groups reinforced each other.

★　★　★

Systems and institutions do not change because of moral appeals. Truth is not their language, and they have no conscience. They respond to pressure. Pressure tactics can shake a system.

Protests and pressure tactics always seem irrational to people observing them from the outside. You will hear them say, "Those protestors don't know what they want!" But such tactics are not designed to make a rational appeal. They are designed to force people to pay attention, and to shake up the status quo. That is what the civil rights movement did with Northern public opinion, and it is what the woman suffrage movement accomplished by protests and political pressure. The systems changed: segregation was dismantled, and women won the right to vote. In neither case was it a victory of truth. The hearts of segregationists and male chauvinists did not change. But the system changed, and that opened the way for hearts and minds to change.

It might be helpful to list a number of practical conclusions about pressure tactics:

1. Since injustice is sustained by systems, activists have to shake the systems through pressure tactics. It is not enough to see the truth and share it with others.

2. Protests and pressure tactics bring their own problems. They can easily become an end in themselves—an exciting, engrossing struggle in which protesters forget what exactly they are fighting for. Some people like the excitement and fail to realize that shaking the system must lead to practical negotiation and compromise.

3. Protest victories will translate into real transformation only if they result in detailed, negotiated change. Sit-ins may succeed, for instance, in shutting down a World Bank conference on global trade. But some people must take the next steps to reshape the rules of the world economy. Having shaken the system, they have to work with the system to bring about negotiated change.

4. Community development makes a great pairing with pressure tactics because it builds up local resources and provides an alternative to the system. After pressure tactics have run their course, the community will be there to negotiate a new approach.

5. Community development and other practical follow-ups require plenty of patience and spiritual maturity. Some people grow frustrated by the partial results and slow pace; they veer off

into ranting against evil in the abstract. Successful community development—indeed, all activism—needs a foundation of spiritual strength as well as a constant renewal of spiritual resources.

6. Activists need to keep truth at their personal center, and truth as a constant companion, while they use pressure tactics. The movement must not leave truth behind in favor of a concentration on tactics. Otherwise the movement can lose its focus.

Even as the civil rights movement used pressure tactics, Martin Luther King Jr. kept a moral appeal at the center of the movement. He always sought to respect the human beings who stood across from him in the battle. "Don't get panicky," he said in an impromptu sermon to a crowd of several hundred angry neighbors who gathered at his home immediately after it was bombed. "Don't do anything panicky. Don't get your weapons. If you have weapons, take them home. He who lives by the sword will perish by the sword. Remember that is what Jesus said. We are not advocating violence. We want to love our enemies. I want you to love our enemies. Be good to them. This is what we must live by. We must meet hate with love."

One reason that the civil rights movement endures as a moral symbol for change is because it had Martin Luther King Jr. at its center. When he died, there was no one to replace him—nobody with his stature who held that kind of conviction. Without it, pressure tactics soon became stale and unproductive.

STAYING POWER

BOB MOSES ENTERED THE CIVIL RIGHTS MOVEMENT at twenty-five. He was a slender, quiet, bespectacled African American who had never spent much time in the segregated South. Moses had nearly completed his Ph.D. in philosophy at Harvard before his father's health made him step out of school. He took a job teaching high school math in New York City, but he came south to Atlanta in the summer of 1960 to work as a summer volunteer at Dr. King's SCLC offices.

Moses had an almost eerie calm about him. When he spoke, it was in a voice so small that people had to strain to hear. In some indefinable way, he was different from anybody else in the movement. Other student volunteers suspected he must be a communist. They actually reported their suspicions to King, who met with Moses in an attempt to discover whether he was a danger to the movement.

The SCLC turned out to be a less impressive outfit than Moses had expected. Essentially it was a church office with three employees: King's secretary, the director of the SCLC and a student volunteer for SNCC. Moses made himself busy, joining student picket lines around Atlanta and helping to lick stamps for funding appeals. When SNCC suggested he travel through the Deep South on Greyhound buses and recruit student delegates for SNCC leadership conferences, he jumped at the chance.

SNCC had nobody at all representing Mississippi, so Moses headed there. In the Mississippi Delta, he met Amzie Moore, a gas station owner and tough World War II veteran who had remained unintimidated by the violent, racist atmosphere of the Delta. Moore sympathized with Moses' desire to recruit students from Mississippi, but he was more interested in getting SNCC to bring students to Mississippi. He considered SNCC's goal of desegregating lunch counters insignificant. Real power went through government, not lunch counters. Moore thought SNCC students should help register local blacks to vote. Since blacks were in the majority in most Delta counties, voting could change everything.

Moses caught the idea and began to promote it within SNCC. He went back to teaching school in the fall, but over the next year he spoke to other SNCC volunteers of his hopes for Mississippi. Although Moses typically didn't say much, and what he did say was often so philosophical it was difficult to apply, SNCC volunteers began to look to him for wisdom. The fact that he seldom attended the organization's long-winded strategy sessions only increased his reputation.

While Moses was quietly promoting voter registration, other SNCC students got caught up in the Freedom Rides of 1961. These began when a small, integrated group from the Congress of Racial Equality (CORE) set out to ride buses through the South and test its segregation laws. The group was attacked and beaten in Alabama, their bus burned on the highway near Birmingham. Suddenly they were national news. SNCC students jumped into the fray, fearlessly volunteering to replace the original riders when the violence overwhelmed them. SNCC students in turn were attacked and savagely beaten in Montgomery, Alabama. The issue became a furious political battle between Alabama officials, who refused to defend the bus riders, and federal officials, who insisted they must. Eventually they reached an agreement: scores of student riders were allowed to take buses to Mississippi, where they were arrested and imprisoned. Both federal and state officials were glad to have the students in jail, out of sight and out of news headlines.

By the time school let out and Moses got back to Mississippi, the Freedom Rides had stirred up such racial tumult that Amzie Moore wanted to wait awhile before trying to register voters in the Delta. Instead, Moore encouraged Moses to go to McComb, Mississippi, supposedly a less volatile place. Moses had not been there long before he stirred up a hornets' nest. While accompanying three would-be voters to register at the Amite County courthouse, he was arrested and jailed for "interfering with an officer in the discharge of his duties." When he got out of jail two days later, Moses went back to the courthouse to try voter registration again. This time he was attacked on the sidewalk by the sheriff's cousin. Though badly bleeding from head wounds, Moses got up off the sidewalk and calmly led his party into the registrar's office. "We can't let something like this stop us," he said. "That's the whole point."

According to the story that spread throughout the county, Moses had clasped his hands and looked to heaven during the assault, saying, "Forgive them." That was not quite true, but it accurately conveyed the way in which Moses' stubborn, quiet nonviolence was seen. Moses got under white people's skin, and he gave black people courage. He calmly stood up to segregationists in small towns where a black could get killed for acting "uppity." Shots were fired into houses where he stayed. A local farmer who attended voter registration classes was murdered. As more students were drawn to Moses' side, they suffered increased violence too. It was an intoxicating combination for idealistic young people: the suffocating, terrifying racism of Southern small towns, ready to kill "outside agitators," and the unruffled, fearless Moses.

Historian Taylor Branch tells of an incident in the summer of 1962 when the SNCC office in Greenwood, Mississippi, was attacked by several carloads of armed men. Moses was elsewhere, conducting a voter registration drive, when he got a panicky phone call from the SNCC office describing white men getting out of their cars, holding guns and swinging chains. Though it was after midnight, Moses set off for Greenwood in his car. When he arrived in the predawn darkness, he found the office door smashed open and the office ransacked. Nobody was there. The other SNCC volunteers had escaped unharmed through a back window and over the roofs of adjacent buildings, but Moses had no way to know that. The next morning when the escapees hesitantly crept back into the smashed office, they found Moses sleeping inside. The legend spread of a guy so cool he could bed down in a room a lynch mob had just left.

Moses kept at it—jailed many times, threatened more, shot at a few times. He gradually convinced more and more local blacks to ignore racist threats and try to register. Local whites responded by assaulting and arresting blacks who even dared approach the courthouse in the daylight, while harassing, threatening, beating, shooting at and fireballing them under cover of night. As more blacks tried to register, the white response grew stronger. Soon the national media appeared, and various celebrities too. The Kennedy administration, trying its best to act sympathetic to black concerns and yet not upset local officials, all Democrats, was dragged into action by the media attention.

Some SNCC leaders devised a plan to ramp up the voter registration campaign even further by recruiting hundreds or thousands of white college students from the North. Thus far, SNCC was almost entirely run by a small, idealistic cadre of young Southern blacks, veterans of a lifetime of segregation. Nearly all were poor. Nearly all were products of the African American church. They sang gospel songs, they took turns standing up to preach when they were in jail, they readily cited Bible verses and prayed. Gospel activity was in the lifeblood of SNCC.

Some in SNCC feared the involvement of huge numbers of naive, privileged white people from the North. They knew that such intruders would change the culture of the movement. Others insisted, however, that SNCC alone could not do the job. Voter registration would get nowhere, they said, unless the battle was raised to another level.

Moses was unsure which side to take. He worried that some of the white students would be hurt or even killed, and SNCC would be responsible. He vacillated until word came of the murder of a black truck driver, a man Moses had convinced to testify in a racist murder. Moses felt responsible for the man's death, since he had talked him into taking a public stand. "We can't protect our own people," he said and threw his weight behind Freedom Summer of 1964.

Freedom Summer was the high point of SNCC. Hundreds of white, Northern students came. They created intense national publicity and intense local resistance. Three SNCC volunteers were murdered in Philadelphia, Mississippi. Black churches were burned if they cooperated with SNCC. Many would-be voters were turned away from registration, but many successfully registered. For the first time, the FBI got involved in civil rights, trying to crack the Philadelphia murders. SNCC helped to form the Mississippi Freedom Democratic Party, an alternative to the whites-only Democratic party. Through all the turmoil and smoke, one simple idea got planted in the nation's conscience: every citizen should have the right to vote. In Mississippi it was an idea so radical that until that summer, few had even dared to whisper it.

It was a thrilling summer, but the tension, fear, exhaustion and excitement, plus the sheer size of the endeavor, were too much for a small organization that ran on a shoestring and liked to argue out every move. Just as some had feared, differences between white and black proved virtually irresolvable. So did differences between male and female. After the summer's elation, SNCC tried to come back to earth and found itself unable to do so. They had always operated as an informal democracy. Now questions arose over who had the right to vote. If a white girl from Boston had endured a summer of fear in Mississippi, did that give her a voice equal to a black man from Talladega who had spent his whole life under segregation? And what about the older, simpler Mississippians who had risked their lives to house and feed the students and go down to the courthouse to register? Did they have a vote in SNCC, or was it strictly for better-educated students? The organization had lived by its wits and its relationships, with no constitution to guide it. The wits and the relationships proved too weak for the new challenges. They fought over everything.

Bob Moses knew that a good many SNCC veterans were waiting to hear from him. Some would follow him wherever he led, and most would listen carefully to anything he said, but he had always feared the corruption that can come when a leader is raised too high. He stubbornly resisted becoming that leader. He would not speak. The squabbling—often bitter, sometimes sophomoric—continued.

And then without warning Moses did speak, at an SNCC summit meeting in Atlanta. After two days of listening to the interminable wrangling, he suddenly stood up. "I have a message for you," he said. "I have changed my name. I will no longer be known as Bob Moses." He rambled for some time, claiming to be drunk, offering a block of cheese and a jug of wine to his listeners in a sort of parody of the Last Supper. Then he returned to his main message. "From now on, I am Bob Parris, and I will no longer speak to white people." He left immediately.

Eventually he found his way to Tanzania under an assumed name, where he married another former SNCC volunteer and had four children. He taught in a village school. When he finally returned to the United States, he taught algebra. Never again was he active in the movement that had been ready to follow him almost anywhere.

★   ★   ★

I am reluctant to say anything that might be understood to be critical of Bob Moses. I look up to him as a hero. He spent four years of his life in the civil rights movement. For much of that time he put himself at the eye of the hurricane, facing down terror and hatred with amazing serenity. He made great contributions, helping to press SNCC and ultimately the entire civil rights movement toward a focus on voting rights. This strategy would arguably make the greatest single difference in revolutionizing the South. Besides his strategic contributions, Moses' personal example inspired tremendous devotion and courage. Others looked up to him.

In four years Moses accomplished far more than most people accomplish in a lifetime. Nevertheless, I can't help reading the end of
his civil rights involvement with sorrow. He was still in his twen-
ties, and there was manifestly a great deal more work to be done.

Through spectacular pressure tactics and a willingness to suffer,
the civil rights movement had caught the conscience of the nation.
The truth of equality had come to the attention of every American.
The activists had shaken the system, and within a few years the legal apparatus of segregation would be dismantled. But the human
needs for reconciliation between black and white, for rebuilding
schools and governments and churches on nonracial lines, for the
strengthening of African American communities, remained barely
touched. Someone like Moses could have helped a lot.

He had survived the terror of segregationist attacks, but he
could not survive the anguish of watching his movement struggle
and disintegrate. And so he left the movement. He stopped fighting. To hide himself, he even adopted a new name. With Moses
gone, Stokely Carmichael gained leadership over SNCC, and in a
short time he would destroy whatever credibility the organization
still had.

Moses was not, of course, the only one to burn out, just the
most prominent. Constant tension, fear and uncertainty took their
toll on the movement. Mentally and emotionally exhausted, people quit. They went back to school. They got jobs. Probably the
vast majority of those who played an active role in SNCC carried
on for less time than Moses did.

This was a major failing of the civil rights movement, and it is a
common failing of many activist movements. These movements
are intense, and they attract intense people. Idealism and passion
meet up with the obduracy of real life. It can be discouraging and

disillusioning and confusing. Some of the most passionate people burn out and drop out.

The civil rights movement talked about creating a "beloved community," which should have helped to sustain people for the long run. Its beginnings in the black church were full of hymns and prayers. By most accounts, however, the church's faith, hope and love became something of an afterthought as the years went on. SNCC became filled with bitter political conflict—always exciting, but very rarely nurturing. It was in such a context that Bob Moses and many others dropped out.

★　★　★

By contrast, it is worth thinking about the example of Martin Luther King Jr. He lasted thirteen years—more than three times as long as Bob Moses—and only a bullet stopped him. As the adored and reviled leader of the movement, King suffered under extraordinary pressure year after year. He struggled with these pressures, and sometimes he caved in to them, but he found strength to carry on.

Maybe it is hard to relate to King, who is now seen as a saint and is evaluated on a different plane from the rest of us. He was not the only one to stick it out, however. Many did.

To most people's eyes, John Lewis was a very ordinary person. He grew up on a remote Alabama farm without plumbing or electricity. Short in stature, he stammered and struggled with grammar. But he was fiercely determined. The first member of his family ever to graduate from high school, he went on to college and seminary. Though naturally quiet, he worked his way into dramatic confrontations at every stage of the movement. Forty times he went to jail. As one of the original Freedom Riders, he was brutally beaten in

Alabama. During SNCC's most turbulent and vital period, he was
made chairman, largely because his integrity was beyond question.
He was a principal speaker at the March on Washington, where
King gave his "I Have a Dream" speech. While leading the famous
march from Selma to Montgomery he was badly beaten by Alabama state troopers.

Then Lewis was removed from the chair of SNCC in a stunning
overnight political coup. The organization was in turmoil after Bob
Moses left. There were squabbles over its future direction. Nevertheless, Lewis had been reelected to another term as chairman—
and then he wasn't. Long after the meeting seemed to be over and
most people had gone to bed, the election was reopened. At 5:30
in the morning, John Lewis was replaced by Stokely Carmichael.

In the emotional, close-knit, tightly wound movement, it was
like being betrayed by your best friend. Lewis was devastated. "I
thought about the fact that no one had spoken up for me," he later
wrote. "My life, my identity, most of my very existence, was tied up
in SNCC. . . . It hurt more than anything I'd ever been through. I
had always told myself and others that whatever the setback, we
had to keep going, that the road was a long and winding one. But
nothing had tested that belief like this."

> It hurt. It hurt to leave my family. . . . My ego was hurt as well.
> My feelings were hurt. I felt abandoned, cast out. I'm a very
> forgiving man, and I was able to forgive this. But it was prob-
> ably the hardest thing I've ever done. And though I was able
> to forgive it, I have never forgotten it. The pain of that expe-
> rience is something I will never be able to forget."

Nobody could have blamed him if he had disappeared. But
when offered a job in New York with the Field Foundation, a group

that worked for civil rights and child welfare, Lewis took it. "As I rode the train up from Atlanta, I felt more lonesome than I had ever felt in my life. I had lived a lifetime in the past six years, and now the rest of my life lay ahead of me, without a map, without a blueprint."

In 1997 Lewis commented on Charles Marsh's book about the civil rights movement, *God's Long Summer:* "Without prayer—without a spiritual anchor—my involvement in the civil rights movement would have been like a bird without wings."

Lewis carried on, finding other ways to contribute. He joined organizations working for voting rights and community development. Greatly concerned with the black community in Atlanta, he became politically involved and ultimately ran for Congress. He was elected in 1986 and at the writing of this book is still in office. He is sometimes referred to as the conscience of the House of Representatives.

★　★　★

Why did John Lewis last while Bob Moses did not? It would be treacherous to say too much, since so many mysteries are involved. People react very differently to stressful situations. An individual's emotional makeup plays an important role. Under the same conditions, one person will be used up and another will persevere.

I can say this: we need more John Lewises, and we should do anything we can to encourage them. Successful movements depend on people with staying power.

Woman suffrage, for example, took more than seventy years to accomplish. During that period, the United States expanded to the West Coast, electric lights and indoor plumbing became common and automobiles were invented and widely adopted. People were born and died while the movement carried on.

For more than fifty of those years, Susan B. Anthony was a force. Lacking Elizabeth Cady Stanton's wit and brilliance, she was easily caricatured as a humorless schoolmarm. She never married, and she seemed to know only one subject. In fact, her greatest strength seemed to be her persistence. Her devotion to the cause kept it alive through periods of great discouragement.

Though Anthony did not live to see her movement triumph, she became a kind of saint to the women who finally got the vote. They recognized that they stood on her shoulders. When the Susan B. Anthony amendment finally passed the House of Representatives, a spontaneous melody rose up in the packed gallery, sweet women's voices singing Psalm 100, known as the Old Hundredth. It is easy to forget, many years later, what an impossible victory it seemed for them and how deeply it touched them. It depended on the unromantic but persistent Susan Anthony.

It will be so of any truly significant movement. Charisma is a great gift. Brilliant intellect and absorbing communication are almost indispensable. But the one ingredient new movements most easily overlook is staying power.

★   ★   ★

Of all the American activist movements, abolition offers the greatest lessons—good examples and bad ones—of staying power. The movement lasted a long thirty years. Activists who were young when it began had become old men and women by the time Lincoln freed the slaves. Opposing slavery was violent and dangerous nearly all of those thirty years, so abolitionists suffered unusual strain. Few people admired the abolitionists, and many hated them.

Given such conditions, it is no surprise that some fell away from the cause and that prominent leaders abandoned the Christian faith, which had impelled them to care about slaves in the first place. Churches by and large were too cautious to endorse the activists' cause, so abolitionists often found themselves alienated from the church. A good many prominent leaders drifted into skepticism or into one of the varieties of heterodoxy that spread through New England in this period: Unitarianism, Universalism, Theosophy, Transcendentalism.

One should not overestimate this trend, however. Ordinary people cared about slaves because the Bible told them to love their neighbor as themselves. Some lost faith, but continuing in faith was more common by far. So was continuing in activism.

In *The Lane Rebels,* Lawrence Lesick systematically researches the careers of all seventy-five students who left the seminary because of their antislavery beliefs. He was able to gain information for fifty-four of them. Forty-two of these continued in antislavery activities, most as evangelical ministers. Only three were known to have given up their evangelical faith. Those three were quite prominent, however; most notable was Theodore Weld.

The parallels between Bob Moses and Theodore Weld are striking. Weld was slightly older than the other students at Lane and was revered for his intellect. Like Moses, he was strikingly courageous, facing down mobs many times. Probably no one else in the movement spoke to so many people in so many obscure places. Probably no one else had so many women fall in love with him or so many men revere him. Weld seemed immortal.

He did, that is, until he reached Troy, New York, in 1836. He had been working through the cities of upstate New York, adding between six hundred and seven hundred members to the Utica antislavery society in February, and eight hundred to the Rochester society in March. He went to Troy in May expecting the usual opposition. Instead he encountered hostility like he had never faced before. All through May and June, he attempted to carry on a series of lectures, but mobs ringed his lodgings, following him and assaulting him whenever he went out of doors. The church where he had intended to speak canceled his lectures, fearing destructive violence. Other public places were made unavailable. Instead of guaranteeing his right to speak, city officials encouraged the mob.

When Weld finally found another church to speak in, his foes charged up the aisle, throwing rocks, bricks, eggs, sticks—anything. A furious scrum began, with the mob trying to get at him to beat him or drag him into the street, and Weld's supporters holding them at bay. The pushing and shoving and rock-throwing continued all the way home. Twice Weld was hit by flying rocks and badly hurt.

Other abolitionists urged Weld to give up and move on. He was invited to speak to the Rhode Island legislature, an important opportunity, but he declined. He would fight it out at Troy. "Let every abolitionist," he wrote in answer to the invitation, "settle it with himself whether he is an abolitionist from *impulse* or principle—whether he can lie upon the rack—and clasp the faggot—and tread with steady step the scaffold—whether he can . . . fall and die a martyr 'not accepting deliverance.'"

Despite the brave words, Weld finally gave in. The mayor of Troy made an ultimatum: leave the city or be forcibly removed. Weld left. It was his first real defeat, and it seems to have changed his whole direction in life.

The change was not immediately obvious. He went on to New York City, where he selected and trained the Seventy to go out and speak, as he had, all over the North. Weld, however, remained in the New York offices.

In the New York headquarters, he met and eventually married the remarkable Angelina Grimke. It was a celebrity marriage. Angelina was a powerful and charismatic figure herself. She and her sister Sarah were daughters of a well-off South Carolina judge, a slaveholder. The two had come north to escape slavery, which they had learned to hate. Their ability to speak in public, to travel around the country without a protective male and to address even "promiscuous assemblies," mixing male and female, had made them a marvel. Some wondered whether Angelina's independence could be contained within marriage.

The marriage seems to have been reasonably happy. There were children. Together with Sarah, the Welds produced the phenomenal *Slavery As It Is*. But that was Weld's last production. He did not speak anymore. He stayed in New Jersey working on his farm.

Weld never fully explained—and his friends never understood—the changes going on within him at this stage. He stopped attending church. Churches were full of hypocrites, he said; he had no more faith in creeds. Fairly soon he concluded that antislavery societies were hypocritical as well. He dropped out of the antislavery movement and dropped into a profoundly inward, isolated way of life. His image of himself as a pioneering man also suffered, as he failed at farming. Eventually he started a school and found he was good at it. He moved to Massachusetts and ended his days running a school for the well-off children of progressive Boston families.

Weld accomplished remarkable things in the approximately eight years he was active in antislavery work. But he could not sustain it. He lost confidence in the movement, in Christianity, in the church and in himself. By the time the slaves were freed, his participation in the great crusade had been all but forgotten. The movement of abolition continued without him, thanks to stalwart people like Garrison, Wendell Phillips, John Rankin and Lewis Tappan. But Theodore Weld was a very great loss to the movement.

★ ★ ★

Weld's story, like Bob Moses' story, reminds us how psychologically and spiritually hazardous it is to head a movement. The pressures are immense, and they are not made easier by adulation. It is never good when leaders become so far above their colleagues that there is no give and take, no mutuality. Movements ought to avoid putting people on a pedestal or letting them put themselves there. A pedestal is a vulnerable place in a storm.

Lewis Tappan was everything that Weld was not. He had many comrades but no followers. That was for obvious reasons: he was fussy, pedantic and bureaucratic, a New York businessman whose greatest achievement was the invention of the credit bureau.

Tappan had his strengths, however. He could do the tedious work the abolitionist movement required: the editing, bookkeeping, letter writing, planning and organizing. He was extremely capable. As the junior partner in his brother's dry-goods store, he was generous with his money, living simply and donating to all kinds of charities, especially abolition. Fundamentally, Lewis was not an egotist. He cared for the cause and seemed to expect very little of the credit. He got on well with characters as diverse and fractious as Weld and Garrison.

As the new American Anti-Slavery Society gradually found its bearings in the summer of 1834, a number of proslavery newspapers made Tappan their target. Rumors spread that he was being watched and would soon be assaulted with tar and feathers. In July anti-black riots broke out in New York. African American churches and homes were attacked and gutted. The mobs singled out Lewis's home on Rose Street. Lewis moved his family into hiding just before a gang of toughs sacked the house, throwing furniture, doors, window frames and everything movable out the windows and into a huge bonfire in the street. The next night a gang attacked the Tappan brothers' business. The clerks were armed and waiting inside the locked building while a battering ram hammered at the door. At the last moment the militia arrived and scattered the mob.

Other troubles would follow. The Tappan firm went bankrupt in the Great Crash of 1837, at least partly because of a Southern boycott. Spurred by the failure, Tappan invented the first credit rating agency and built it into a successful enterprise. (It survives today under the name Dun and Bradstreet.)

Even more troubling to Tappan was the prejudice he discovered among abolitionists and Christians. In 1834, in the midst of the crisis at Lane Seminary, Lyman Beecher complained to Tappan that Weld and his fellow rebels were encouraging social relations between blacks and whites. It would lead to promiscuity and mongrelization, Beecher predicted. Tappan responded impatiently that "in a thousand years probably all the inhabitants on this continent would be of one color, neither black nor white (both being exotics) but copper colored, the original color of this climate." He didn't care a fig whether the races mixed.

But he was far ahead of his time. In 1835 Tappan began crusading against segregated seating in New York's Chatham Chapel, where Charles Finney preached, for at Chatham Chapel, as at nearly all churches of the time, blacks sat in the upper balconies known as "nigger heaven." When Finney came back to preach in the spring of 1836, he put an immediate end to the integration experiment.

Later Finney defended segregation at Oberlin College by distinguishing between slavery, which he considered sinful, and a "constitutional" distaste for the company of other races, which he thought was merely a matter of personal preference. He was as good an abolitionist as anyone, he contended, but that did not mean insisting that all people worship God from the same pew.

Tappan was deeply dismayed. Finney represented the pinnacle of evangelical holiness for him, and yet undeniably he was prejudiced. Later Finney's New York church chose a proslavery pastor who had Tappan excommunicated, apparently because he tried to start a mixed-race abolitionist group in the church.

"After many years of toil and suffering," Tappan told a friend, "I am reluctantly brought to these conclusions—to this low estimate of the steadfastness of a majority of professed Christian abolitionists—and to the painful necessity of laboring to elevate people of color rather than bring white people to right conduct towards their colored brethren." In other words, he had given up fighting white people's prejudice.

Thereafter Tappan spent more of his time leading Sunday schools, which as missions to the poor were far enough outside the church mainstream to allow the races to mix. He attended black churches a great deal of the time. His loyalty was to the church of Jesus Christ, not to white institutions.

★ ★ ★

Tappan mainly worked behind the scenes, a steady, persistent force. The *Amistad* case is a sterling example. In the summer of

1839, a Cuban ship anchored off the coast of Long Island, New York. A Navy cutter spotted it and, finding it commanded by a motley crew of Africans, took control. A remarkable story gradually came out.

The Africans were slaves who had been captured in Africa earlier in the year, brought to Cuba, outfitted with false Cuban papers, and sold to the highest bidder. While being transported along the coast of Cuba in the *Amistad,* they mutinied, killing some of the crew but preserving two alive to help with navigation. They meant to sail back to Africa, but their two prisoners confused them by sailing east during the day and west at night—effectively going in circles until, out of food and water, they stopped off at Long Island to look for provisions. There the navy found them and arrested the slaves on charges of piracy and murder. They were taken to New Haven to await trial.

The sensational news spread rapidly, but only Lewis Tappan felt compelled to help the Africans. As soon as possible, he journeyed to New Haven to meet with them in jail, arranging for some Yale divinity students to offer regular spiritual instruction and care. He began to orchestrate newspaper articles that were sympathetic to their plight.

At first glance the Amistads, as the slaves became known, seemed to be a straightforward case of slave insurrection. These slaves had defied the law and committed murder. The guilty had to be punished and any innocent bystanders returned to Cuba as slaves.

Tappan haunted the New York docks for days, using a few phrases he had picked up from the Amistads until he found a cabin boy who knew the dialect (known as Mendi) from his days in Africa. Using the cabin boy to translate, he was able to slowly unravel the full story of the Amistads' illegal transport from Africa and their forged papers from Cuba. They were *victims* of piracy and kidnapping; their mutiny was in self-defense.

Proving that to the satisfaction of the courts took two years, eventually going all the way to the U.S. Supreme Court. During that time Tappan suffered extraordinary grief when his eighteen-year-old daughter, Eliza, died slowly of tuberculosis. Even so, he never faltered: raising funds to support the legal cause, finding lawyers, arranging publicity and making sure that the Amistads were well treated. After the courts finally set them free, Tappan helped arrange for the expensive trip back to Africa, sending along missionaries who would work with them in spreading the gospel. For many of the Amistads had come to faith in Jesus Christ during their imprisonment.

The case had been nationally publicized, and through it, the general public came to see the Amistads as heroes and their imprisoners as villains. It was perhaps the first time that Africans had been viewed that way in America. The images of mistreated, captive Africans and cold-hearted, obdurate government officials would be multiplied in the next decade under the Fugitive Slave Law.

Another outgrowth of the Amistad case was the American Missionary Association (AMA), which was launched to help the Amistads return to Africa. Soon, with Lewis Tappan's leadership, the group became an alternative to Christian organizations that compromised with slavery. Most independent organizations such as the American Bible Society or the American Board of Commissioners for Foreign Missions tried to avoid criticizing slaveholders. Abolitionists thought that was sinful compromise, allowing racism to set the tone for the entire church and its missions. The AMA, by contrast, condemned slavery, ministered to black and white alike and would not let slaveholders participate in its organization. With Tappan's entrepreneurial and bureaucratic skill, the AMA flourished. During and after the Civil War it would expand even further, playing a large role in helping freed slaves and providing for their education. Many of the historically black colleges of the South were started during that period by the AMA.

Tappan was a practical man. He was not a subtle thinker, and he lacked the charisma of a Theodore Weld or even a William Garrison. He had staying power, however. He worked hard, and he persisted. Certainly he faced discouragement. His home was wrecked by rioters, his life was threatened, his business went bankrupt. He experienced the failings of his fellow Christians and his fellow abolitionists, including some he greatly admired and liked, such as Charles Finney and Theodore Weld. Like everyone else, he saw very little of the progress that he longed for. He began in the movement as a young man, and he ended it an old man.

Yet he carried on. He maintained his faith in God. He continued to work within the institutions of the church and of abolitionism, but he worked with them by trying new approaches and constantly agitating for change. His staying power was not passive or fatalistic; it was continually hopeful and energetic. These are qualities that are necessary in a movement that hopes to change the world.

Why did Tappan stick? He seems to have been blessed by a dutiful temperament, reinforced around the disciplines of church attendance, Bible reading, hard work, punctuality, honesty and truthfulness. In short, he was a drudge. Dropping out, starting his own cult, declaring himself too good for the run-of-the-mill Christian was simply not a possibility for him. Something should be said for duty and a lack of imagination. Lewis Tappan would be one to say it.

Some people are wired to trudge along and stick to it. Others, often brilliant stars, seem wired to suffer crises, perhaps because they feel so deeply. My point is not to criticize them. My point is that discouragement and burnout are serious issues in any movement that seeks to change the world. We should make a point to admire steady workers like Tappan. As for the brilliant burning stars, we had better think of ways to help them keep their fire for the long run.

★ ★ ★

What conditions make for staying power? One factor is simply pacing. Movements are like marathons, not sprints. People need time to regroup. They need regular sleep and decent food. Lewis Tappan, for all the drama in his life, was sustained by an ordinary work schedule, by a conventional family, by many friends and associates. The same was true of William Garrison, who found joy in his work and in his many friends.

Activist movements do not always allow for conventional lifestyles. For short periods, at least, activists can do without these supports. In some movements, though, people virtually compete for the extremes of danger, lost sleep and overwork. That can't last. SNCC, with its youthful atmosphere of invincibility, is a perfect example. Not only did they fail to take care of themselves, but they competed with each other to be the most reckless. They lived like there was no tomorrow.

If the history of American activism teaches anything, it teaches that there is a tomorrow. There will be lots of tomorrows. We need people who live like they know that.

Activists need a supportive community. They are often tempted to reject the community they came from because they find it insufficiently radical—as happened, for example, when SNCC broke its ties to the black church. Sustaining those relations from both sides can be difficult, filled with tensions and differences. But a wider community can offer activists refuge, love, support and a broader perspective.

When I meet activists, I always want to know about their community. Do they go to church, if they are Christians? What kind of friends do they stick with day by day? Do they have balance and breadth in their lives?

And what about sustaining faith? Very often activist movements have their roots in faith. I always want to ask: what do they do to sustain it? I look for movements that nurture prayer, worship, study and celebration. They will have a better chance to last. On a purely practical level, faith brings staying power.

There are new causes every minute. Plenty of charismatic, passionate people rise up. That's good: we need this passion, this revolutionary agitation. Those who make a difference, though, are usually those who invest a lifetime.

John Perkins went back to Mississippi as a young man, determined to make a difference in the poverty-stricken communities of his birth. He is still there forty years later. The work has been slow, and he has experienced many setbacks. Perkins's deep roots in God and church have sustained him. His solid family life has helped him in times of despair. He has lasted, and as a result he has a legacy of activists sprinkled in poor communities all over the country.

We need more activists who carry on like Perkins. We need to build movements that help people like him to persevere.

THE SEDUCTION OF VIOLENCE

CARRY NATION WAS PERHAPS THE LEAST likely person in Kansas to set off statewide mob violence. An elderly, somewhat portly housewife, she lived in the small southwestern Kansas town of Medicine Lodge. As a devout Christian, she had gained a reputation for her good deeds to the poor of the town. She was active in the temperance movement, joining with other advocates of the Woman's Christian Temperance Union (WCTU) to sing, pray and verbally confront alcohol vendors. Partly due to their persuasion, all seven of the town's illegal liquor outlets had closed down.

Why exactly Nation went on to more violent methods has been much debated. Thirty years before, her beloved first husband had died of drink after just two years of marriage. Perhaps his demise had festered in her mind until it produced the violent actions of the spring of 1900.

For whatever reason, one day Nation drove her horse and buggy the twenty miles from Medicine Lodge to Kiowa, where she used rocks and pieces of brick to smash three liquor joints in a single day. Her technique was simple: she would break anything that she could—mirrors, furniture, glasses, bottles. She was strong enough and bold enough to do a lot of damage.

After Kiowa she stayed home for six months, but in the fall of 1900 she traveled to Wichita, entered its finest hotel and demolished its bar. She was arrested and jailed for three weeks. On coming out, she immediately began smashing again and was rearrested.

From Wichita she went to the small town of Enterprise and spent two days in an orgy of smashing as well as hair-pulling, pushing and wrestling.

By this time, Nation had gathered considerable notoriety—and many allies. She carried her growing crusade to the state capital, Topeka, just as the Kansas State Temperance Union (KSTU) was gathering for its annual convention. The KSTU was divided over Nation and her violent tactics. Many prohibitionists, especially men, found her approach unacceptable. But Catherine Hoffman, a cultured woman who had worked with Nation in Enterprise, told the convention that she had helped Nation because "the men would not do it, [so] we women did it. . . . I do not believe in war, I did not believe in violence. But I tell you, this is a revolution that is coming on us in this state. . . . That is what Mrs. Nation signifies today—action, revolution."

★ ★ ★

To understand this celebration of violence and revolution, it helps to know something about Kansas. From its very beginning Kansas was a progressive state. The majority of the farmers who settled its vast prairie opposed slavery; many had come to Kansas prepared to fight with guns to keep out proslavery settlers and interlopers from Missouri.

Along with abolitionism often came a cluster of other beliefs, such as the advocacy of free public education and opposition to alcoholic beverages. That combination may seem surprising today, when many liberal and progressive people can hardly get through the day without their glass of wine. In the nineteenth century, however, many progressives felt deeply the dangerous antisocial effects of alcohol. Conservatives, on the other hand—those mainly concerned with business and often identified with the South—typically favored the brewers, distillers and distributors who made a living off the sale of alcoholic beverages. Our modern categories of liberal and conservative don't quite fit the nineteenth century.

Temperance forces were strong. In 1880, Kansas voters (all male) passed an amendment to the state constitution outlawing the manufacture and sale of alcoholic beverages. Only Maine had done anything like it.

This great victory for the dry forces turned out less decisively than the voters expected, however. Kansans learned that enforcing laws against drink can be harder than passing them. (Forty years later, the whole nation would learn the same lesson with national Prohibition.) In many communities, officers of the law showed quite tepid interest in stopping the sale of liquor. In some towns and cities, fines for the illegal sale of alcohol became an important source of revenue for local government. This perversely ensured that the sale of liquor would continue, because city governments came to depend on the regular collection of those fines.

Thus the end result of outlawing liquor was this: liquor remained available most places, though technically illegal. This state of affairs frustrated temperance advocates no end. Many were women whose home life suffered from drinking but who had no political rights to effect change. They could file complaints but would get no response. Sometimes temperance women saw an active connivance of winks and nods between local officials and the alcohol interests; other times they saw mere indifference, an unwillingness to take alcohol seriously. For whatever reasons, alcohol remained quite available in much of Kansas. "All felt that the state was a seething, surging volcano of suppressed emotion," a contemporary commentator wrote, and "that a mighty conflict was inevitable."

★ ★ ★

When Carry Nation appeared at the KSTU convention in Topeka, a tidal wave of enthusiasm met her. "I tell you ladies," she said, "you don't know how much joy you will have until you begin to smash, smash, smash. It is wonderful." Her harshest words went to those who thought they should stick to moral appeals. "Moral suasion!" she cried. "If there's anything that's weak and worse than useless it's this moral suasion. I despise it. These hell traps of Kansas have fattened for twenty years on moral suasion."

During the month of February 1901, mobs of women and men followed Nation on planned forays to smash Topeka's saloons or "joints." Unable to restrain thousands of Nation's supporters or to establish law and order, the mayor ordered all liquor establishments to close. Even so, Nation's army kept on smashing. Most of the violence was to property, but a few injuries occurred in the pushing and shoving.

Nation's violent crusade spread throughout Kansas. In at least fifty towns, people broke up saloons, and in some places serious injuries occurred. By the end of February, the violence had abated. And sadly for Nation's cause, by the end of the year the sale of alcoholic beverages was as robust and visible as ever.

Today Carry Nation is usually remembered with amusement: a

stout grandmotherly woman leading mobs of devout Christian women to smash furniture in Kansas dens of iniquity.

To the people involved on both sides, however, there was nothing funny about it. A great deal of property was destroyed. For the women who did the destroying, a fundamental line was crossed. When else have hundreds and thousands of respectable women—Methodists and Baptists and Disciples of Christ—gone on a rampage like that? When else have people from such backgrounds spoken of the joy of smashing?

★ ★ ★

Nation's crusade suggests the attraction of violence. Most American activists begin with nonviolent principles. At some point, though, many experience powerful temptations to take up violent means. To the stymied activist, violence offers a sense of cleansing purity, a release from the tension of frustrated ideals. Activists come to violence when they are frustrated beyond reason.

I experienced this firsthand during Vietnam protests. All through those endless debates about tactics, nobody suggested violence. It would have been unthinkable. We considered ourselves to be on the side of peace. "All you need is love" would be our theme song. However, seeing that the war did not melt quickly away, frustration grew, and a violent fringe emerged. That violence, though very small compared to the violence of the war it opposed, undermined the movement. I myself stayed away from protests when I knew that some people would be throwing rocks through windows or at police. Of course, these violent acts were done by a small minority, and they were usually decried by the movement leaders themselves. But without a doubt, the people throwing rocks (and even blowing up research labs, as happened at the University of Wisconsin) were part of the antiwar movement, and their reputation as dangerous radicals kept many people from joining the movement against the war. In a battle for American public opinion, violence is almost always counterproductive.

You can see the same temptation at work today, in animal-rights terrorism and abortion-clinic bombings. Ecoterrorists burn ski lodges and smash labs. The more passionately a cause is pursued and the more difficult progress becomes, the more likely that at some point violence will begin to fascinate certain activists. Every movement to change the world must take stock of this reality.

★　★　★

One can make a case for violence, of course. South Africa's African National Congress (ANC) practiced nonviolent protest against the apartheid regime up through the 1950s. But after being banned from public existence, the ANC chose violent means to bring down the government. In 1961 a military wing was launched, called *Umkhonto we Sizwe,* meaning "Spear of the Nation." The ANC bombed, murdered and sabotaged for three decades, and in the end it brought down apartheid.

Palestinians who launched the second intifada in 2000 made a similar calculation. Some think their choice of violence over Gandhi-like passive resistance was disastrous for their cause, but the story is still playing out.

Going deeper into history, theologian Dietrich Bonhoeffer decided to fight the Nazi regime by helping with the assassination of Hitler. The plot failed and Bonhoeffer was executed, but most people think of him as a hero and a martyr.

The Civil War ended slavery by extraordinarily violent means—hundreds of thousands of deaths. Yet nearly all abolitionists cheered, including trenchant believers in nonresistance, such as William Lloyd Garrison.

My interest in this chapter is not to debate whether violence or nonviolence is better. My personal belief is that most times—and nearly all times in a democracy like America—nonviolent means are much more effective. Yet I admit that sometimes violence is necessary. Perhaps the war against Hitler and the Nazis has been overused as an example, but for a reason. It makes a strong case for violent means in extreme cases.

I am not going to argue for or against the philosophy of nonviolence. My concern is more immediate, for the way in which violence creeps into an activist movement as a result of frustration. Often enough, a movement that has strong nonviolent convictions ends up contemplating violence just because they are tired and discouraged. That can undermine or even destroy the movement.

Carry Nation's violence does not fit that description. It was embraced by a large contingent for a time and then dropped, completely and decisively. It did no lasting harm to the temperance movement, and no lasting harm to the liquor interests either. You could call it a quirk of history—though an interesting one, certainly.

The Civil Right movement, however, is a more complicated case. What began with the Montgomery bus boycott and the Freedom Rides was determinedly nonviolent, built on Jesus' call to his disciples to "turn the other cheek" and "love your enemies." Despite beatings and even murders, the movement kept to that commitment.

But it was not easy. From the very first days, civil rights activists insisted that protestors train themselves in nonviolence. They practiced having people hit them, shout racial slurs at them, kick them and knock them down so that when real confrontations came they would be prepared not to retaliate. Martin Luther King Jr. was quite aware that by marching and protesting and trying to register to vote, blacks would arouse white anger and violence. When that violence came, it would be very tempting to strike back. King always carefully calibrated his protests so as not to accentuate a cycle of violence.

Despite the determination of King and others to proceed nonviolently, the possibility of violence dogged the movement. The ten years between 1955 and 1965 seemed like a lifetime to those involved. The activists were beaten, jailed, threatened and verbally abused, not once but dozens of times. And what results did they see? After ten years of nonviolent protests, black people still could not vote in much of the South, and in some counties brutal white people continued to do as they pleased, even murdering blacks with impunity. To the activists, these were not abstract facts but realities they confronted almost daily. They became weary and frustrated.

As the years went by, the commitment to peace weakened. Malcolm X and the Black Muslims jeered at those committed to nonviolence. Civil rights leaders feared they were losing influence as younger blacks impatiently demanded results.

In June 1966, James Meredith—the same man who had integrated the University of Mississippi in 1962—decided to set off on a one-man protest march across Mississippi. On the second day of his solo journey, he was ambushed by the side of the road and shot. Civil rights leaders from across the nation converged on his hospital bed in Memphis, pledging to take up the march from the spot where Meredith had been forced to quit it.

The march proved to be a nightmare. Stokely Carmichael had

taken over leadership at SNCC only a month before, and he saw the march as a chance to assert bold leadership. He managed to attack and aggravate the most moderate black leaders until they left. He then set up a running battle with King and his supporters over the slogan "Black Power." The marchers loved chanting those words, which sounded potent. But King was sure the slogan would be misunderstood by whites, who would see it as accentuating the separation and hostility between white and black. The tension between King and Carmichael was obvious to everyone on the march. Evening rallies sometimes degenerated into competing chants: Black Power! (Carmichael) vs. Freedom Now! (King). Even if Carmichael did not quite advocate violence, he was not outspokenly opposed to it either. He pointedly welcomed groups that carried guns. In his rhetoric and appearance, he liked to appear threatening. He acted deliberately unfriendly to white allies, telling them they were not wanted. The march ended with an unsatisfying whimper and a rising suspicion that the movement spent more energy arguing about slogans than working together for common goals. Most of all, it left a suspicion inside and outside the movement that violent confrontations would be coming soon and that younger blacks were eager to provoke them.

After that march in 1966 the smokescreen of violence never completely left civil rights. This muddied its appeal to ordinary Americans, who sympathized with Rosa Parks's desire for a seat on the bus but not with Stokely Carmichael's vision of black power. Without widespread support, the movement became bogged down. The frustration of not meeting goals made the movement and the black community more prone to violent rhetoric, if not violent actions. Race riots broke out in many cities, and the movement was not able to give a clear response. Its struggles in the years before King's assassination, and its struggles since, are at least partly due to the lure of violence and the movement's muddled response to it. The movement endured violent assaults, even murders, and never struck back. But the mere rumor of impending violence upset both the movement's internal unity and its attraction to the general public.

Violence has a symbolic significance that dwarfs everything else.

★　★　★

The odd fact is that American movements rarely start out thinking about violence. I am quite sure that the earliest protestors against abortion never dreamed they would eventually be condemned as bombers and murderers. I doubt very much that people protesting cruelty to animals imagined in the early days that their stance on terrorism and firebombing would be front-page news.

In some movements, violence never becomes an issue. The fight for women's rights has never to my knowledge taken up violent means. Aside from Carry Nation's brief career, violence had very little to do with temperance. Still, often enough, violence becomes an issue for activists, one they find themselves unprepared to face. The abolition of slavery is the outstanding example.

From the beginning, abolitionists pledged themselves to radical nonviolence. They did not favor slave rebellions, did not countenance political coercion and would not free the slaves by force even if they could. When the abolitionists themselves were mobbed and beaten, even killed (as in the case of editor Elijah Lovejoy), they would not fight back or retaliate.

But they found their commitment to peace increasingly difficult to maintain. Slaveholders attacked them whenever they could. Violence toward escaped slaves or free blacks knew few limits, and abolitionists felt helpless in the face of it.

The town of Ripley, Ohio, sits on the Ohio River with a broad stretch of Kentucky immediately in view across the shallow river. Rev. John Rankin moved to Ripley from Kentucky in 1821 specifically because he hated slavery. He built a house on a hill overlooking the river, and each night he put a light in the highest window. That light, visible far up and down the Kentucky shore, became legendary. Escaped slaves knew that if they could make it across the river to Rankin's house, they would be smuggled north. Hundreds and perhaps thousands of slaves made it to safety thanks to Rankin, his family and their local allies.

White Kentuckians fought back. Rough characters would cross the river supposedly looking for escaped slaves. Sometimes they would simply kidnap free blacks, tie them up and carry them back to Kentucky by force. The law in Kentucky made it all but impossible for these kidnapped men and women to get free.

In 1837 James Fox and three companions came to Ripley looking for an escaped slave. Instead they found Eliza Jane Johnson, a thirty-two-year-old black woman with a husband and five children who had lived in Ripley for three years and belonged to the Ripley Anti-Slavery Society. Seizing Johnson and beating her into submission, Fox threw her on a horse and raced for the river. Half a dozen people from Ripley pursued, catching two of the kidnappers. But Fox got Eliza Johnson across the river and deep into Kentucky. She slept that night on the dirt floor of a basement jail in Washington, Kentucky.

In the morning, James Fox's father, Arthur, came to see her. With one glance he shook his head and said that, though she bore a striking resemblance to his escaped slave, she was not the one. This, however, did not set Johnson free. According to Kentucky law she had to remain in jail for two months to see if anyone else claimed her. After that the sheriff could run advertisements in local newspapers in search of her owner. At the end of a year, the sheriff could sell her and use the proceeds to cover the cost of her incarceration. The presumption of the law was that any black person was a slave and must belong to someone.

John Rankin rode to the Washington courthouse to try to free Johnson, but he failed to persuade a judge. He and his Ripley allies launched a political campaign to put pressure on Kentucky, and eventually this bore fruit when Johnson's case was brought to the floor of the Ohio House of Representatives and a motion condemning her capture was passed. A few weeks later, a Kentucky circuit court ordered her freed. She was given a hero's welcome in Ripley, having been imprisoned for five months. But the memory of her experience left a legacy of fear around Ripley.

While Johnson had been in prison, another attempt had been made to brazenly kidnap a black dock worker. Only because a group of sympathetic whites had rushed his kidnappers had he been able to leap into the river and escape.

From that point on and for years to come, antislavery activists near Ripley stayed on edge, ready to fend off attacks on their neighbors and friends. They had guns—nearly any farmer in America did—and they were ready to use them. They had many repeated encounters with armed slave catchers who demanded to search their homes for escaped slaves. Hostility grew with familiarity, so that a state of "ready to go to war" existed in that part of Ohio and Kentucky many years before actual warfare began. The constant threatening interplay could turn violent in a breath.

In that kind of environment, nonviolent principles are easily eroded.

★ ★ ★

Ripley was unusual. In most parts of America, proslavery and antislavery factions had much less direct contact. Abolitionists heard threats of violence only from a distance; the plight of the slave was something they read about in a newspaper.

That began to change drastically in 1850, ten years before the Civil War, with the passage of the Fugitive Slave Law. The new law was intended to end an offense that Southerners found intolerable: that slaves could escape into the North, where local authorities would make no attempt to return them. Under the new law, all citizens were compelled to aid in the recapture of slaves, under severe penalty of law. And the standards of evidence for stolen property were set very low. Someone apprehended as an escaped slave could call no witnesses to defend himself. The law presumed on the side of the slave catcher.

Antislavery activists complained bitterly that this law forced them to aid a deeply immoral practice. Furthermore, the law violated Northern sovereignty, for it encouraged armed posses from the South to roam the North hunting for escaped slaves, almost as a law unto themselves. Inevitably these posses sometimes attacked free blacks and tried to take them South. Inevitably whites resented the Southern intrusion into their communities. Pitched battles were fought. Innocent and not-so-innocent people were injured or killed. When the federal government used its might to return captured slaves to the South, as they did in Boston in the face of massive resistance, it was bound to create feelings of outrage. Every time the Fugitive Slave Law returned escaped slaves to their masters, it created new abolitionists. The slave power became a reality to many Northerners after 1850, for they saw it operating in their own neighborhoods.

Partly because of the violence they witnessed personally, the abolitionists' opposition to slave rebellions became muted. This had always been a dodgy point for abolitionists. They proclaimed themselves nonviolent, and they urged slaves to hold to the same standard. But what if slaves followed the common American practice of defending themselves? What if, like Nat Turner, they fought for their freedom? Abolitionists had a hard time condemning such slave rebellions. They knew that the average American believed that people who were kidnapped had every right to fight their kidnappers to the death. Did not black people, kidnapped into slavery, have that right?

For many years this question remained theoretical. Abolitionists were against violence, and that was all they needed to say. The Fugitive Slave Law and the violence that followed threw open these questions again. If Yankee farmers could defend their homes from the slave catchers and use guns to order them off their farms, then what kept African Americans from defending their lives and families?

★   ★   ★

Then came Kansas. Blacks were hardly involved: it was a competition between white men to determine what kind of state they would have, proslavery or free-soil. The conflict soon became violent, with small-scale skirmishes and full-scale battles fought between settlers, especially over elections.

Thousands of New England farmers emigrated to Kansas, armed and ready to defend it as a free state. Thousands of "border ruffians," mainly from neighboring Missouri, flooded over the border to vote in Kansas elections, and later to fight. Fifteen years earlier, Missouri had violently propelled Mormon settlers out of their state, and they expected to do the same with the Free-Soilers in Kansas. Missouri's senator David Atchison wrote to Jefferson Davis with his plans: "We will be compelled to shoot, burn & hang, but the thing will soon be over. We intend to 'Mormonize' the Abolitionists."

A lean, wizened, Bible-quoting John Brown attended the American Abolition Society's June 1855 meeting in Syracuse, New York, pleading for money to buy guns for Kansas settlers. He won support from most of the delegates, including Frederick Douglass, the escaped slave who had hitherto hewed to Garrison's policy of absolute nonresistance.

Lewis Tappan was astonished. "Would not one Uncle Tom do more good by his pious submission to God . . . than a score or a hundred men who should act exactly opposite?" Later he wrote Joseph Sturge, an English abolitionist, "In this community I am almost alone in inculcating the duty & sound policy of maintaining peace. Rifles, it is said, are peace weapons. It is hard to withstand the multitudes."

In November 1855, fifteen hundred Missourians marched on the free-soil stronghold of Lawrence, Kansas, where one thousand armed men waited for them behind barricades and earthworks they had hurriedly thrown up. The governor of Kansas intervened and talked them out of a fight. The peace was temporary, however. In the spring an eight-hundred-member posse of Missourians poured into Lawrence, destroying its two newspaper offices, burning its hotel and the home of its free-soil governor, and ransacking stores and homes.

Meanwhile in Washington, D.C., Massachusetts senator Charles Sumner gave a two-day address on "the crimes of Kansas" and was subsequently accosted, beaten senseless and nearly killed by South

Carolina congressman Preston Brooks. Southern newspapers and politicians lauded Brooks for his deed. Back in Kansas, an infuriated John Brown led a nighttime raiding party that slaughtered five proslavery settlers in their homes on Pottawatomie Creek.

★   ★   ★

In the increasingly violent atmosphere, few asked questions about what John Brown had done in Kansas. Almost certainly abolitionists would have been appalled at his conduct, had they known about it. The point is, they had stopped wanting to know. Frustration and anger had changed the direction of abolition.

Brown was by all accounts an astonishing character, something like an Old Testament prophet Elijah. He seemed to take no account of others' opinions but to operate from an internal mainspring that kept perfect time with itself. Blacks like Frederick Douglass noticed he was completely natural with them, treating them as his equals without any trace of self-consciousness. That was very rare in an America where black and white almost never met as equals. Brown had a boldness and simplicity others could not touch.

So it was that he got people's ear after Kansas, when he devised a scheme to start a massive slave uprising in the South. His plans were completely secret, worked out with great earnestness. They fit into the theoretical mutterings in favor of slave rebellions, only with this difference: Brown had a plan to make them happen. The Northern abolitionists whom he asked for help had no direct experience of war, had never even fired a shot in anger. They gave him their secret support—in money and in words, though none of them would put their bodies into the plan.

Brown wanted Frederick Douglass to serve as the new president of a slave republic they would form from rescued slaves in the Appalachian Mountains. Douglass admired Brown enough to meet him secretly at a deserted quarry in Pennsylvania. There they engaged in argument for two days, Brown explaining his plan to Douglass and urging him to take part. In the end, Douglass declined.

So Brown, with a small gang of supporters, went to war. He turned out to be utterly incompetent as a military leader, attacking Harpers Ferry, Virginia, in a completely inept raid. He managed to get several of his men and a few innocent bystanders killed before he was captured.

Then while waiting to be hanged, Brown did what he did best: he talked. His eloquent Bible-quoting words were printed all over America. To the South, they made a ghoulish exhibit of how eager Northern abolitionists were for the South's bloody destruction. To the North, Brown's words conveyed the very image of an Old Testament saint, willing to give his life for the cause of the slave.

Of course, some abolitionists still maintained that Brown had been wrong to take up arms against the South, but those sentiments were overwhelmed by the belief that John Brown was a martyr to a just cause. The popular song "John Brown's Body," which would later accompany Union soldiers to battle, gives some idea how much the old man's death was idealized. Such glorification of violence would have been impossible when the abolitionist movement began, but thirty years of frustration and failure had left their mark. Violence had become not just a temptation but a sign of sacred commitment.

Thus it was that the nonviolent abolitionist movement led the way into the bloodiest war in the history of the United States.

★   ★   ★

From a pragmatic point of view, it is hard to prove that nonviolence is more effective than violence. Gandhi has his advocates, but so do freedom fighters. Had John Brown led a successful raid at Harpers Ferry, had he raised a guerilla movement of freed slaves, I would find it harder to criticize him.

You can make a case that some institutions and governments are so hardened, violence is the only way to break them open. You can make that case in regard to Southern slavery. John Brown, in fact, made that case without apology. I can respect him for that, though not for the careless way in which he pointlessly murdered some and led his followers to pointless deaths.

What I find regrettable is the way the rest of the movement stumbled into supporting violence, or pretending not to see it, without ever discussing their reversal of principle. They had begun their crusade holding very firmly to nonviolent principles. Garrison and his many disciples actually grew increasingly committed to peace and nonresistance. They might fairly have said, "We were wrong. The South will only give up the evil of slavery by force, and slavery is so evil it demands that force." But they never really had that discussion. Most abolitionists tried to have it both ways, clinging to their nonviolent principles in theory while singing the praises of John Brown. They fell into supporting violence without counting the cost. So did America, one might say, for both North and South marched enthusiastically into the Civil War. Abolitionists had been a guiding light to America's conscience in regard to slavery, but they failed to provide any guidance regarding the slaughter of America's brothers and sisters.

I don't mean to be hard on the abolitionists, only realistic about the seduction of violence. Activist movements may go on for many years and endure many frustrations. In those frustrations, violence may begin to appeal.

Elements of the civil rights movement felt that pull, particularly SNCC. So did the temperance movement, when Carry Nation began to smash. The woman suffrage movement could easily have been drawn to violence, too, if they had been forced to wait still longer for the vote. Today, movements against abortion, against animal cruelty and against environmental degradation have fringe elements who engage in violent protest. In each case, that fringe minority has the potential to darken the way ordinary people perceive the movement.

Considering this, I believe that the possibility of violence should be addressed, publicly and candidly, long before it becomes an issue. I think movements should be prepared to correct some of their own members—to publicly warn people who flirt with violence, lest some take passionate rhetoric ("abortion is murder" comes to mind) into action. Activists need to be proactive in heading off the possibility of violence. They need to think ahead.

In the case of John Brown, few really wanted to know what he had done or what he was thinking of doing. Most preferred not to ask too many questions. Maybe they could not have stopped John Brown anyway. We will never know, because they did not try. Lewis Tappan could hardly find someone to take his concern seriously. Abolitionists ought to have paused for a candid, deep discussion of violence. They ought to have taken time to make their convictions clear.

The threat is not that a nonviolent movement will turn officially toward violence. The threat is the seduction of a fringe minority. When people are aroused and frustrated, they are willing to overlook ambiguously violent threats. They lose the energy to confront someone who might, or might not, be harboring violent plans, because in frustration they almost wish for violence. That is how John Brown was enabled to raise money and develop supporters right in the midst of an outspokenly nonviolent movement.

PARTY POLITICS AND THE PROPHETIC ALTERNATIVE

Suppose that your passion is for endangered species. You want to protect each intricate creature, whether Siberian tiger or snail darter. Lacking any endangered species in your backyard, you look for the best way to act on your passion.

You have choices. You can join groups that publicize environmental dangers. You can contribute money to buy wildlife preserves. You can chain yourself to a logging truck or picket a business that wants to build on a wetland. You can write letters to your congressional representative or dump a load of manure in front of the nearest office of the Environmental Protection Agency.

At some point, though, you may decide all this agitation is mere "sound and fury, signifying nothing." To protect endangered species you must have power, and to get power in a democracy you have to elect somebody to office. Such thoughts will lead you to consider politics.

People who seek to change the world usually have mixed reactions toward politics. In politics they find a mismatch between their own idealism and the compromises and deals that politicians make in seeking votes. Activism is driven by truth. Politics is often driven by special interests, half-truths and sound bites.

As truth-driven people, activists don't always have patience with voters who care only about their small, selfish interests. But good politicians do have such patience. In Chicago the very popular Mayors Daley, father and son, made their worldwide reputation on the basis of street repair, parks and jobs. Politics invariably involves such practical matters. That leaves little room for idealism.

Politics may be sordid or mundane, but it holds the promise of getting something done. Activists don't want to spend their lives fruitlessly. Do you want to change the world or just talk about it?

★   ★   ★

I am not asking whether an activist should vote. I take it that people living in a democracy should do their civic duty by studying the issues, forming opinions and participating in elections. The larger question is whether activists should go beyond that. Should they dedicate themselves to political action as the best way to further their cause? And if so, how?

Regarding these questions, as in so many things, the abolitionist movement set the pattern. No other issue divided abolitionists so much as politics.

William Lloyd Garrison, the most influential abolitionist of them all, was a natural extremist on this point. He reviled politics—an odd thing, since by temperament he was so well suited to it. Garrison loved a fight, never losing his temper but causing countless others to lose theirs by his barrage of rather personal, needling criticism. He had a way with words and could frame an issue to make his most extreme opinion seem sensible. Garrison had started out his publishing career writing for political papers. By the time he took up abolition, however, he had become resolutely antipolitical.

At the founding of the American Anti-Slavery Society in 1833, most abolitionists shared Garrison's antipathy toward politics. Why not? They were a tiny minority with an extremely unpopular point of view, widely viewed as fanatics who wanted to interbreed with other races. Politics held little promise for a minority with that kind of reputation.

The abolitionists' strong suit was their moral argument. Slavery is sin, they said, and slaveholders must repent. What does politics have to do with that? If you change the law and set slaves free, you have not changed slaveholders' hearts. The early abolitionists hoped to challenge the very character of America. Politics didn't offer much leverage for such fundamental change.

The abolitionists' view of politics began to shift because of two developments. First, abolition became a little less unpopular in the North, so that abolitionists began to see some hope of gaining majority support. Second, abolitionists realized that a moral argument alone would never convince Southerners to give up their slaves.

Garrison responded by taking his original moral analysis deeper. The more he probed, the more he saw that slavery was a symptom of a more profound moral disease—the pathological need to subject other people to your will. Once you began to look, you could see this everywhere: in the family, where men made women their slaves; in government, which forced citizens to conform and obey; in church, where the clergy mandated obedience to their rules. Everywhere, people forced their will on others, and what was slavery but an extreme instance of this universal human tendency?

This analysis led Garrison even further away from politics. You could hardly fix people's coercive tendencies through coercive laws.

Garrison and his followers instead grew interested in utopian universal reform—change that would affect every aspect of life, not merely slavery. To abolition they added causes like peace, religious liberty and women's rights. Many refused to vote, since the government used coercion; some refused to pay taxes. The most thoroughgoing formulation of their point of view was "no human government." Human government—one person in authority over others—stood against God's government. Until God ruled the hearts and minds of Americans, there was no hope of ending slavery.

Few Garrisonians took his philosophy to its logical conclusion, by which it would be wrong for parents to discipline children or for police to restrain murderers. Garrison was not a systematic thinker but an intellectual gadfly who picked his arguments and ignored inconvenient questions. That is not to say he had no method to his extremism. By consistently taking the moral high ground, by sticking to pure principles, Garrison mounted a clear, sustained attack on slavery for thirty years. Leave reasonableness to others; you knew where Garrison stood.

As the slave power grew more obstreperous and slave-catching posses prowled the North for escaped slaves, Garrison and his followers increasingly saw American politics as decadent and immoral, a compromise with sin. The ultimate symbolic act came at a Fourth of July celebration in 1854, when Garrison ceremoniously burned the Constitution. It was "a covenant with death," he said and his slogan was "No Union with Slaveholders." Long before Southern slaveholders decided to secede from the Union, Garrison was arguing for the North to secede from the South and escape its sin.

If I had lived in 1840, I doubt I would have sided with Garrison. By temperament I tend toward pragmatism, compromise and moderation. But the history of abolition has made me reevaluate my tendencies. Looking over thirty years of abolitionist agitation, you cannot doubt Garrison's effectiveness. His idealism might seem unrealistic and fanatical, but he made a clear witness. And he stuck with it, in season and out of season. Nobody made a greater difference in turning America away from slavery.

Garrison's example makes a strong case for activists who stay away from politics. If they can accept derision and contempt, making their case eloquently and persistently, they can have a mammoth impact for the truth.

I think we need more prophets. But let me warn you: prophets are not easy to get along with.

Garrison's radicalism was the main reason why the American Anti-Slavery Society split in two in 1840. "A great many abolitionists were dismayed," writes historian Merton Dillon, "to find their cause so freely labeled 'radical,' 'dangerous,' 'fanatical,' and themselves tagged as 'incendiaries,' 'madmen,' and worse. Such words did not fit their own self-image, for they generally pictured themselves as respectable citizens and as staunch defenders of orthodox religion and traditional values." By this time, Garrison had staked out radical positions on so many issues that other abolitionists felt they had to separate themselves from him.

The fighting issue was whether women could serve as officers in the American Anti-Slavery Society. Garrison, committed to women's rights, insisted they could. He was effective at packing the annual convention with supporters and winning the vote. His opponents, led by the Tappan brothers, withdrew to form another antislavery organization. They might have learned to live with

women officers, but they could not tolerate an organization dominated by Garrison's radicalism.

The question of politics, not women's rights, was the cutting
edge of their concern. That very year abolitionists would launch a
political party and run a candidate for president. The abolitionist
split of 1840 represented a division between two kinds of activism:
Garrison's, which stood outside the realm of politics, prophetically
condemning America's sins; and everybody else's, which hoped
that slavery could be eliminated before the kingdom of God came
in its fullness. People who put a premium on results were drawn
toward politics.

★   ★   ★

Wendell Phillips, the great orator and Garrison supporter, complained in 1844 that "as fast as *we* . . . make abolitionists, the new
converts run right into the Liberty Party, and become almost or
wholly hostile to us." He thought this was because of "the strong
leaning of our national character to politics."

That seems right, and it is an important point. Phillips could
give a great sermon on the evils of slavery, appealing to the idealism in America's character. Mixed with American idealism,
though, is a strong streak of pragmatism and a fundamental instinct toward democracy. Therefore, most of Phillips's converts
didn't stick to his prophetic idealism. They looked around for a
practical solution and fell naturally into politics.

Americans are the same today. Activists may catch consciences
with prophetic words, but there will be a strong tendency to con-
vert those ideals into a practical political program. For that reason
alone, activists need to think long and hard about politics. It will
continually surface in different forms for any American activist

movement. If activists do not stay "pure," like Garrison, they are likely to go first of all in the same direction that abolitionists went: into a pure, single-issue political party.

As patriotic Americans, most abolitionists believed in voting almost as much as they believed in attending church. As the 1840 election approached, they realized that both the Whig and the Democratic candidates for president were pledged to sustain slavery. It galled them—but they still wanted to vote.

Thus the Liberty Party came into being, with James Birney as its candidate for president. Not even his most optimistic supporter expected Birney to win anything, but at least he gave abolitionists the possibility of voting in a morally upright way.

Birney stood for moral rectitude. The Liberty Party nominated him not because he was a great politician but because he was a man of substance and high morality. Time and again he had followed his conscience, even though it cost him dearly. He had been an aristocratic, dissolute plantation slaveholder until debt drove him to take up law in the town of Huntsville, Alabama. There, transformed by a renewed Christian faith, he helped represent the Cherokee nation, which was about to be thrown out of Georgia and sent on the Trail of Tears, and became active in many charitable causes. Convinced that he should do more for slaves, Birney gave up his law practice and became a full-time worker for the American Colonization Society. He helped organize shiploads of freed slaves to go from New Orleans to Liberia.

Antislavery activities made Birney increasingly unpopular in his Alabama home. He had once been mayor, but now the pressure drove him to move to Kentucky. There, with the help of Theodore Weld, he came to see the futility of colonization. He decided to publish an antislavery newspaper. When that venture met with vi-

olent opposition, Birney moved his family across the river to Cincinnati. Several times mobs in that city destroyed his printing press
and threatened his life, but he stood up to them bravely. He gained
a reputation for great personal dignity and righteousness, which is
why the Liberty Party chose him.

The Liberty Party stood for a single issue: the abolition of slavery. It took no stand on other issues. A vote for Birney was a protest vote, essentially—a way to state your heartfelt convictions in
the voting booth.

It was pure, yes, but it won no elections. In 1840 Birney got a
mere 7,000 votes out of 2,400,000—about three-tenths of 1 percent. That might be considered beginner's bad luck, but in 1844,
with a great deal more organization, Birney got 62,300 votes—
more than the first run but far fewer than one would need to wield
any political power. Only in the state of New York did the Liberty
Party make a difference, for it drew off enough votes from Henry
Clay to throw the state's thirty-six electoral votes—and the presidency—to James Polk, a Tennessee supporter of proslavery interests. Abolitionists were pure in voting for James Birney, but their
votes managed to help a candidate from the slave power. The Liberty Party withered and died.

★   ★   ★

Such is the fate of single-issue parties in America. They do not
make headway. Yet idealistic activists have a powerful impulse to
launch single-issue parties.

The temperance movement followed a similar path. They began
with organizations and lodges, making speeches, launching newspapers and falling to their knees praying in bars. They saw alcohol

as a moral issue and believed that moral persuasion was the only way ahead.

When prohibitionists failed to sway society, they began to think of politics. In 1869 the Grand Lodge of the Good Templars—an influential teetotaling group—proposed a mass convention of all like-minded people to consider political action. Observing that "the existing parties are hopelessly unwilling to adopt an adequate policy on this question," the convention launched the Prohibition Party. Their first presidential candidate ran for office in 1872.

They found, however, that very few voters would abandon the existing parties to "throw away" their vote. For three elections— 1884 to 1892—Prohibition Party votes leaped from about 10,000 votes to 150,000 in 1884; 250,000 in 1888; and 271,000 in 1892. These were heady moments, but at their peak they represented about 2 percent of the total votes cast. That was simply not enough to sway national policy.

Political parties succeed by emphasizing a number of different issues rather than just one. Often enough, these coalitions don't make much rational sense. Today, for example, the Republican Party thrives by drawing together evangelical Christians with their moral concerns, businessmen who want lower taxes and government policies that favor business, neoconservatives who believe in an aggressive, idealistic foreign policy and libertarians who want less government regulation in everything. These different factions are often at odds. Libertarians, for example, want the government to leave us alone, regardless of our moral choices; evangelicals want to see the government restrict abortion and pornography. Yet somehow the party manages to blur the disagreements, emphasizing common ground.

Single-issue parties do not—cannot—assemble such coalitions.

Furthermore, the American winner-take-all approach to elections grants very little governmental power to second-place parties, let alone third-place parties. Losing with 10 percent of the vote is losing completely.

Rick Gaber notes that third parties "give the otherwise ignored, used, abused, betrayed, disgusted, disappointed, frustrated, victimized, insulted, and/or outraged voter a chance to cast a vote without feeling dirty afterwards, a reason to go to the polls AT ALL in the first place, and maybe even to come out of the voting booth feeling GREAT!"

Because activists long to feel great about voting, third parties will always crop up. We have them today: the Green Party, the Libertarian Party, the Peace and Freedom Party, and other parties so obscure as to be utterly unknown to the general public. There still exists, in fact, a survivor to the Prohibition Party. Such parties offer only a temporary satisfaction to activists' urge for political involvement. Sooner or later—usually sooner—activists go on to other forms of political involvement.

★   ★   ★

When activists grow frustrated with "pure" third-party politics, they often look to form less-than-pure coalitions. So it was when the Free-Soil Party grew out of the Liberty Party. For two election cycles, abolitionists had been happy enough to vote in a virtuous way for James Birney. By 1848, however, they had seen that the Liberty Party would never be more than a symbolic gesture.

Antislavery feelings had been steadily increasing in the North—especially resentment against the South's slave power. Some antislavery Democrats and Whigs began to buck party policy and speak out boldly against slavery.

Party discipline was breaking down. In 1842 Representative Joshua Giddings was censured by his Whig colleagues for defying party policy and raising the issue of slavery in Congress. He resigned his seat, went home to Ohio and ran for the seat he had just given up. He won the special election overwhelmingly. From that point on, he was a Whig with a difference, a "Conscience Whig."

Three years later in 1845, Democratic Representative John Hale defied his party's commitment to the annexation of Texas as a slave state. He was promptly censured and read out of the Democratic Party. Ordinarily that would have ended his political career, but a group of rebellious Democrats supported him for reelection, in defiance of the party leadership. Hale made some rip-roaring antislavery speeches that convinced Liberty Party members that he nearly measured up to their standards of purity.

People began to believe that a new national coalition was possible, combining pure abolitionists with rebellious factions from both Whig and Democratic parties. What brought these groups together was not love for slaves but a sense of outrage about the slave power meddling in Northern affairs. They agreed mostly on one thing: they wanted the expanding western frontier to be free of slavery—free soil. In some cases they were frankly racist: they wanted to keep slavery out of the West because they wanted to keep blacks out of the West.

The abolitionists were aware of this racism and aware, too, that many of their potential allies had no beef with slavery as long as it stayed in the South. They recognized the lack of morality in much Free-Soil ideology. But they were hungry for success, and they thought they could outsmart their rivals.

So when a call came to convene in Buffalo, New York, in August of 1848, many of the Liberty Party members decided to attend. So did a sizable contingent of Conscience Whigs, outraged that in June their party had nominated for president Zachary Taylor, a slaveholder and plantation owner from Louisiana. The Barnburner Democrats, a faction from New York State, came to Buffalo in great numbers too. They were ready to boost their champion, ex-president Martin Van Buren.

★   ★   ★

The Free-Soil convention in Buffalo was a boisterous and complicated event. Consider Joshua Leavitt, an abolitionist who played a major role there. Leavitt was an evangelical Christian, an ordained Congregational minister who had served as editor of several of the best-known abolitionist publications. As a leader in the Liberty Party he was convinced that something new must be done.

Like virtually all abolitionists, Leavitt went to Buffalo with a great deal of trepidation "that under the pressure of a deep desire to stay the spread of slavery," as he wrote, "and amid the excitement of an immense assembly, our members would be hurried away to abandon our platform of principles." He particularly feared Van Buren: "The Liberty party *cannot* support him, without deliberately giving the lie to all our own declarations for fifteen years past." He vividly remembered how strenuously Van Buren had worked as president to send the *Amistad* captives back into slavery in Cuba, because Leavitt had worked hard alongside Lewis Tappan to free them. Van Buren had been the worst example of Northern politicians kowtowing to the slave power. Had he really changed? Leavitt doubted it. Van Buren appeared to be nothing more than a typical politician, trimming his sails to get votes but showing no core convictions that would oppose slavery.

On the train to Buffalo, however, Leavitt met several Van Buren supporters who surprised him with their "tone of candor and respect" for the Liberty Party. At Buffalo, Leavitt found an amazing atmosphere of jubilation and chaos: perhaps twenty thousand people had come, overwhelming all the public facilities. They met in a gigantic tent erected in a public park, cheering speaker after speaker, while in a nearby Universalist church, a core of leaders thrashed out a plan. Leavitt was part of this behind-the-scenes negotiation, helping to write a series of platform resolutions that he felt covered the Liberty objectives. When the platform was read to the sweaty mob in the big tent, "every sentence, every paragraph was cheered into its legal existence."

Nominating a candidate for president promised to be more difficult. Most Liberty Party leaders wanted to support John Hale, the New Hampshire Democrat who had burned his bridges through strong antislavery speeches. Hale was not anxious to run for president, but he authorized Leavitt and others to use his candidacy as a bargaining chip. Leavitt held a letter from Hale that he was instructed to use only if abolitionist concerns were met. By the letter, Hale removed himself from the competition.

Leavitt did use the letter. He convinced himself that Van Buren was the man to support. Van Buren supporters claimed that the grand old man had changed his mind and would remove slavery from the District of Columbia. They hinted that he had come around to a thoroughgoing antislavery position. Caught up in complex and exciting negotiations, Leavitt believed these assurances. In fact, he ultimately stood before the huge, restless tent audience to back Van Buren. Leavitt was an imposing figure, silverheaded, well over six feet tall, with flowing beard. He moved that the nomination of Van Buren be unanimous. He gave a lengthy, dramatic speech that he considered the best of his life, bringing tears and shouts of joy from the throng. "We have gained everything, lost nothing," he would later write to the remnant of the Liberty Party. "The Liberty party of 1840 is not dead. It has been expanded into the great Union party." Afterward Leavitt threw himself into the campaign for Van Buren.

In the November election, however, results were disappointing. Van Buren got more votes than James Birney had, but it still amounted to only 10 percent of the vote. Free-Soil won nothing. And the cost, contrary to Leavitt's heat-of-the-moment assessment, was considerable. It became clear during the campaign that Van Buren would do nothing to oppose slavery. The Free-Soil platform made some vague indications that the government should stop supporting slavery, but it said nothing against slavery itself, nor for the rights of blacks.

Leavitt was like a man who had just learned the rules of poker, getting into a game with card sharks.

It is true that years later the Free-Soil coalition would become the Republican Party, which would elect Abraham Lincoln to the presidency and fight the Civil War that freed the slaves. One can say that the outcome, in the long run, was good. And one can point out that abolitionists weren't getting anywhere with the Liberty Party. Leavitt was right to say, "We lost nothing."

However, nobody should mistake that for a bold and successful venture into politics. Abolitionists joined an impure coalition because they wanted political power to free the slaves. It didn't work out as they had planned.

Some people get juiced up by the excitement and competition of politics. It gives them the sense—often false—that they and a small circle are in the know and in control. That is what breeds "inside the Beltway" thinking. Some people find the political oxygen intoxicating. I think Leavitt did.

Added to this is the sense—also often illusory—that politics has the power to bring tremendous change. Experienced politicians have a keen sense of the limitations to their power. From the outside, however, and especially to the novice, politics seems to hold the world in its hands.

Activists who seek to change the world are vulnerable to this attraction. Some (but not all) find that politics quickens their pulse. They can get sucked in, even if they started out scoffing at the corrupt political scene.

Perhaps activists more than most others can stumble badly in politics. Activists aren't always humble. Like Leavitt, they think themselves smart and morally good, and they often look down on compromised politicians. It is true that politics rarely rewards intellectual brilliance and almost never rewards moral excellence. But successful politicians bring their own capacity and cunning, and it never pays to underestimate them.

Therefore, coalition politics calls for caution. Activists who become involved in politics do sometimes see good results. Just as often, though, they end up disillusioned and embittered by politics. Often it is their own fault.

As I write, the religious right is engaged in an experiment with coalition politics. The movement started out mainly as a protest against abortion and other signs of decadence in American society. Seeking results, however, the movement aligned itself with the Republican Party, which includes other factions quite disinterested in the moral causes of evangelicals. With the election and reelection of George W. Bush, the religious right seemed to become politically powerful. It celebrated electoral success with hope for great things to be accomplished. As I write, most of those hopes have been disappointed.

Activists can stay away from politics and maintain a strong prophetic stance just the way Garrison did. They may also become active in political parties, either pure third parties like the Liberty or the Green parties, or coalitions like the Free-Soil or Republican parties. The history of American activism doesn't rule out any of these choices. It does suggest that success does not come easily, quickly or cheaply—if at all—through any mode of action.

APPLYING POLITICAL PRESSURE

THERE ARE OTHER WAYS FOR AN ACTIVIST to become political. What about cultivating politicians who are already in power? That was very much a part of Martin Luther King's strategy for change, after the brash new administration of John Kennedy reached out to him with a seductive embrace.

The civil rights movement began with bus boycotts and lunch-counter sit-ins, and not a whiff of politics. It never occurred to King, nor indeed to any civil rights leaders, that they might have friends in high places. Politicians as they knew them were racist governors and volcanic county sheriffs. You did best to keep them out of the picture, not draw them in. The national government was far, far away, and in living memory had not showed evidence of caring about black people.

In 1960, however, John F. Kennedy gave African Americans hope. The new president's youth, social ease and optimistic out-look suggested that he would oppose racial injustice. These hopes were questionably realistic. True, Kennedy had none of the racial habits of older Americans. But he also had little experience with African Americans, and he was a cold-blooded politician with no intention of disrupting the racial status quo under which he had been elected with the support of a solid, segregated South.

Kennedy reached out to King because he hoped to keep civil rights quiet. He played a double game with King: suggesting that he was on his side, promising federal action in exchange for King's cooperation, but actually doing almost nothing to help.

King bit on the bait, perhaps because it fit with the worldview he had grown up in. King was the son of a pastoral dynasty. He was accustomed to decisions made in private by a leadership cabal. For him, the messiness of marches and boycotts required an adjustment in thinking. To arrange settlements behind the scenes, to interact with movers and shakers in private, made natural sense to him.

Kennedy and King met once early in the 1960 presidential campaign—a cordial but inconsequential exchange of views. After Kennedy's election, they met again in the spring of 1961. King had not been invited to an earlier March meeting of civil rights leaders. White House officials thought him too edgy, too difficult to control. King wrote asking for a private meeting with the president, but he was turned down. White House aides finally decided that a secret meeting with the president's brother Robert would do. If King followed the rules and kept the event out of the newspapers, they would conclude that he was malleable.

The meeting took place in a Washington hotel, and Kennedy aide Burke Marshall did most of the talking. He tried to convince King that the federal government could do very little to oppose segregation. What they could do was work through the courts for voter registration.

King was all affability. He agreed with Marshall's emphasis on voters, though he stressed that there was no reason to quit other kinds of agitation. His quiet demeanor and his lack of edge pleased Kennedy's aides, and they managed to have King "accidentally" bump into the president during a tour of the White House. Robert Kennedy, who was attorney general, also gave King private phone numbers for two Justice Department aides, Burke Marshall and John Seigenthaler. If any of King's voter registration workers needed help, they could call day or night.

From the point of view of King and his fellow civil rights leaders, this was enormously hopeful and significant. African Americans had absolutely no power outside their churches. They had grown up knowing that they could not make eye contact with whites, that they had best mumble a quiet "Yes sir" when talked to. Now they could say they dined cordially with the attorney general and had private phone numbers for top government officials. The unimaginable power of the federal government was on their side.

From the point of view of the Kennedy administration, they had gained an inside line on the civil rights movement, a chance to influence it and keep it from creating troublesome confrontations. If the contacts could be kept out of the newspapers, they would not disturb the administration's relations with Southern politicians. Kennedy wanted to appear sympathetic and concerned for African Americans, but he primarily hoped to minimize disruptions in the status quo. Race relations were changing, but he wanted them to change peacefully, slowly and quietly.

Within months, this secret and unstated compact was tested when a small group of idealistic pacifists calling themselves Freedom Riders set off on a bus trip across the segregationist South. The Freedom Riders, who were both black and white, intended to travel together and violate segregationist practices both in bus seating and in the rest stops along the way. They had been warned that they might be killed for this, and they had taken the precaution of informing the Justice Department in Washington of their plans. They, too, had been given phone numbers.

In Alabama the Freedom Riders were hijacked by a white mob. One bus was torched along the highway, its Freedom Riders severely beaten. The other escaped that mob only to find another waiting in the city of Birmingham. Those Freedom Riders were severely beaten too. Many made their way to the home of Rev. Fred Shuttlesworth, a Baptist pastor known for his fearlessness. From there they called the Justice Department. The man who took their call, John Seigenthaler, promised that the Department of Justice would see that their right to safe interstate travel was protected.

The story of what happened next is very complicated. It involved multiple mobs and multiple beatings, both in Birmingham and in Montgomery. When the original Freedom Riders gave up the battle, a group of SNCC students arrived unannounced from Nashville to take their place. For the first time, the infamous Bull Connor, a brutal Birmingham police chief, burst on the national scene. The entire nation was caught up in the drama, which unwound over more than a week.

This was precisely the kind of out-of-control event that the Kennedy administration had wanted to prevent. Instead they found themselves pulled in by their telephone numbers.

Taylor Branch recounts one mass meeting at the Kingston Baptist Church. Shuttlesworth came in to an adoring, spillover crowd and announced, "I talked to Bob Kennedy six times." He "recounted in detail all the courtesies and solicitude he had received that day from the nation's chief law enforcement officer, a white man. Interrupted by a whispered message, he told the audience, 'Excuse me, I have a long-distance call from Bob,' rushed off, and came back with a full report," in which he quoted the attorney general extensively.

Not only did the attorney general find himself talking to excited black preachers, he found himself personally cajoling Greyhound officials to get a driver willing to take the Freedom Riders to their next destination. The president himself tried to intervene by calling on his personal friendship with the Alabama governor, but instead found himself snubbed—the governor's secretary said the governor was fishing.

Rather than peering down on the local conflict as though from Mount Olympus, the Kennedy administration was caught in its octopus arms. Word spread rapidly among whites that the Kennedys were "nigger lovers" and that they had stage-managed the whole conflict. For segregationists raised on the rhetoric of states' rights, even the rumor of the federal government's involvement waved a red flag.

The Kennedys wanted to ease out, but events conspired against them. When they sent John Seigenthaler to Montgomery, he blundered into a mob that had come to beat up the Freedom Riders for a second time. Seigenthaler ended up in the hospital with a concussion. That made it inconvenient for the administration to back away from "a local matter." A few days later the Freedom Riders, along with hundreds of Montgomery believers, were trapped in Ralph Abernathy's Brick-a-Day First Baptist Church. A mob was outside advancing against inadequate police defenses, and it seemed entirely possible that a massacre was about to occur.

Once again the phone lines were busy as King called Robert Kennedy for help. The attorney general was forced to call on federal marshals to protect the church, which further confirmed his growing notoriety with segregationists. The Kennedy administration secured police protection to get the Freedom Riders out of Alabama but stood by while Mississippi police arrested them and sentenced them to long prison terms.

★ ★ ★

That is how it went, and not only with King. Bob Moses, leading
SNCC's work for voter registration in Mississippi, also had direct-
access phone numbers with the Justice Department. Living under
constant threat of violence, he had many opportunities to use
them. He would call to report that a local sheriff had beaten and
threatened people trying to register to vote. But although the Justice Department promised protection for voter registration, they
never provided it.

The federal government had power and plenty of legal authority.
The right to vote was fundamental, and it was painfully obvious
that local and state authorities were determined to deny it, by violence if necessary. For the Kennedy administration, though—as for
most governments—politics took priority, and politics encouraged
them to maintain the status quo. They promised help but always
backed away from confronting local authorities. Their betrayal was
one factor leading to Bob Moses' growing despondency and eventually to his leaving the civil rights movement.

By the time of the great protests in Birmingham, Alabama, in
1963, a certain amount of wariness had developed. King had been
invited to Washington again, but apparently only with the intent
of insisting that he fire one of his top aides and friends. Stanley
Levison was white and, the White House insisted, a communist
spy. King said he found that hard to believe: could they give him
proof? The White House insisted that he take their word for it. As
a matter of fact, they had no proof, because FBI chief J. Edgar
Hoover refused to give it to them. He was playing his own game of
political manipulation against the White House and his enemy
Bobby Kennedy.

The Kennedy administration kept up the pressure on King. King listened but resisted. Trying to exert pressure of his own, he made a private phone call to the president, begging him to propose civil rights legislation such as had been promised in the Democratic platform. Kennedy said such legislation would be futile; it would never pass. Kennedy preferred to pursue black-white relations by hosting a White House gala for a large cross section of the African American elite. King declined the invitation to attend.

As long-planned protests in Birmingham approached, both sides fell out of contact. The White House let it be known that they considered such protests disruptive and counterproductive. Desperate for a victory, the civil rights leaders gambled on confronting the city known as the meanest in the South.

It did not go easily. Fred Shuttlesworth had promised more than enough demonstrators if King and his team came to Birmingham. However, demonstrators proved scarce, and they grew scarcer as day after day Bull Connor arrested them and put them in jail to stay. Birmingham was a very scary place to face police who had a well-earned reputation for brutality. Protestors who were arrested could lose their jobs, with little hope of getting another one with a white employer—and nearly all employers were white.

To inspire more marchers, King himself had to march and go to jail and stay there without posting bail. (There was no money to bail out the others, so elementary fairness dictated that King stay.) While in jail he was inspired to write his famous *Letter from a Birmingham Jail*. Almost completely isolated from the outside world, he slept on metal slats. Singer Harry Belafonte contacted Robert Kennedy to complain, but he got no sympathy. King had gone against the Kennedys' advice, and now he was on his own.

Meanwhile King's wife, Coretta, was frantically calling the

White House. President Kennedy finally returned her call and expressed his sympathies. When King was shortly thereafter granted a phone call to his wife, she eagerly told him of the conversation. He seized on it, telling her to immediately inform Wyatt Walker, his top aide. Walker proceeded to publicize the fact that Coretta had been called by the president. The incident showed how eager King and his supporters remained to grasp at the help of the White House. They had ample evidence of the Kennedys' political cynicism, but they continued to look to them hopefully.

When King bailed out of jail, he found that volunteers were scarcer than ever. Though large crowds filled the churches where he spoke, he could coax only a score of marchers willing to go to jail. Finally on May 2, King made a decision: he would allow and encourage minors to participate in the illegal marches. Since adults were unwilling or unable to give more, they would sacrifice their children.

It was a fateful decision that reflected dire circumstances. Children who were arrested would be expelled from school, with no second chances. Adults who encouraged them to march might be arrested for contributing to the delinquency of a minor, charges that might stick and result in long prison terms. Further, the civil rights leaders were violating the trust of many parents, who thought that children should be kept out of harm's way.

It was a desperate gamble, and the gamble paid. The children jubilantly streamed out of Sixteenth Street Baptist Church by the hundreds, were arrested and taken to jail. Trying to repel them, Bull Connor used fire hoses and police dogs. Suddenly the attention of the national news media was back on Birmingham. Photos of dogs biting young African Americans and of fire hoses rolling youngsters down the street captivated America. Day after day the young marchers continued to come forward by the hundreds, and some adult Birminghamians, inspired by their courage, went out to march with them. Black opposition to King's strategy evaporated.

The White House could not stand aloof from the crisis any longer. The administration sent Burke Marshall from the Justice Department to negotiate a settlement. Now he was calling on King, shuttling from him and Shuttlesworth and Andrew Young to white officials and businessmen who refused to meet personally with black leaders. The negotiations went nowhere, but protestors were energized to know that Washington had noticed them. Ralph Abernathy told a huge crowd at Saint Luke's Baptist Church, "Today I sat in a room with one of the top men in the Justice Department, who paced the floor, couldn't sit down, changed from chair to chair." He told the crowd they had white people tied in knots. They shouldn't worry about their children in jail, because he would call Burke Marshall about their safety. "And if he doesn't do anything about it, I'm gonna call *Bobby*. And if Bobby doesn't do anything about it, I'm gonna call *Jack*."

Other people did call Jack. The impasse in Birmingham threatened to spiral into real violence, leading to martial law imposed by either Governor George Wallace or the federal government. Kennedy did not want that: it would undermine him politically. He began to make private phone calls, as did members of his cabinet, in an effort to bring the demonstrations to a close. King for the first time—for the first time!—called publicly on the president to take a stand against segregation. With pressure from Burke Marshall, the "big mules" of Birmingham—prominent businessmen who ran the city behind the scenes—decided to compromise and agree to end segregation in the city's business district. In a press conference President Kennedy endorsed their hopes for a settlement. In the

end, to get hundreds of demonstrators out of jail, Robert Kennedy
had to secretly raise $160,000 in bail money from private sources.
A tenuous settlement was reached.

It was clear that, without the federal government's involvement,
no agreement could have been reached in Birmingham. It was also
clear that the federal government acted out of concern to quell a
public relations disaster rather than out of concern for anyone's
civil rights. King put it well in an older-and-wiser address to a post-
settlement meeting at Saint John's Baptist Church in Birmingham:
"The United States is concerned about its image. When things
started happening down here, Mr. Kennedy got disturbed."

He had lost his earlier hopeful optimism about the Kennedys
caring about black people. He understood that the government did
not react to private conversations unless those were supplemented
by public pressure.

The civil rights movement under King learned that power to
change the world could not be borrowed from friendships in far-
off Washington. It did not really matter whether you had their
phone numbers. Power to change the world began and ended in
the churches and streets and buses of places like Birmingham and
Montgomery and Jackson. The thrill of reaching Bobby Kennedy
on the phone was just that: a thrill. Kennedy, like all politicians, responded only to political pressure.

Access matters as an entry point. Unless you have bargaining
chips, though—credible threats, credible promises—you can't
move a politician.

The principle remains the same whether in national politics or
in a local city council. Activists who know people in power can
sometimes get things done. But to do so, they need to give the
powerful a motive to move.

★ ★ ★

I experienced this just two years ago. I had joined a neighborhood committee that was fighting against the development of some open space near my house. Though I live in a densely populated area of a midsize city, there is a lovely, wild strip of land just a block away. Most people don't know it exists because it's tucked in a valley you can't see from any road. It's a lovely refuge, a place for short walks and a haven for wildlife. A developer bought a portion of it and wanted to build houses.

When I joined my neighborhood group, they had been working hard for some time, without results. I did not have much time to give to the effort, but I volunteered that I knew the mayor, because our kids had gone to school together. I said I would be glad to call him up and see if he would like to take a walk to see the area.

I did just that. Mike Martini is a friendly guy—most politicians are—and I made a very low-key pitch. I said that I knew he was getting phone calls and letters about the Paulin Creek property. "Would you like to go for a walk with me and see what people are talking about?" He said he would.

On the day in question it was pouring down rain. But Martini was up for a walk, so we headed off up the hill. I could tell by Martini's few comments and his body language that he was prepared to tell me there was nothing he could do. That changed as we walked the property. He didn't say much, but I think he was stunned. He had no idea such a beautiful place existed inside the city limits, unspoiled. In the downpour it looked all the more wild and scenic.

Within a week Martini had contacted the key players in the city and county governments and worked out a deal to buy out the developer and join the whole parcel into a perpetual wild park. He knew how to get it done, and he had credibility and clout. He deserves a lot of credit. So do the members of the committee I joined, who had identified the threat and set out to stop it. I did hardly anything, yet I very much doubt the land would have been preserved had I not known Martini and invited him to take a walk.

Note, however, that Martini didn't do it because he liked me. He went for the walk because he liked me. He took action because it was a beautiful piece of property, an obvious asset to the community, and because there was money available through our county's open space district to buy the necessary property. Other activists had done the spadework to develop that district and pass a quarter-cent sales tax to buy open space. Most fundamentally, Martini did it because he represents a community that cares about preserving open space. Local politics were on the side of what we wanted to do.

All the pieces had to be aligned, or it would have been a no-go. Nevertheless, it was access—friendship, actually—that started everything moving.

I take a couple of lessons from this, and they are the same lessons you can draw from Martin Luther King Jr. and the Kennedys. If activists want political clout, it helps to know people. Useful friendships are usually developed long before an issue comes to a crisis. If you know someone in government, you will find it far easier to get results when the crisis comes.

Lesson number two, though, is that politicians only do what they perceive to be in their interests. It's not friendship that gets something done in the political scene—though friendship helps. What moves politicians is the next election.

They hate bad publicity. They love good publicity. They love to please people who can deliver votes or volunteers or a platform from which to campaign. They also pay attention to people who can make their lives miserable by protests or other bad publicity.

Martin Luther King Jr. only got action from the Kennedys when he disregarded their advice and fomented protests that captured national attention. He could only do that because he had a strong base in the organization he led and the churches that supported it, and in the thousands of African Americans in Birmingham who would put their lives on the line.

Activists need to bring assets to the political process. Sometimes research helps, to show politicians or government officials the validity of your position. Sometimes excellent presentations help, to show the logic of your views. It helps to understand how government works, so you do not ask officials to do the impossible but apply your efforts to people who can actually accomplish what you ask.

The greatest asset, though, is a group of people who can threaten uncomfortable protests or promise encouraging support; who can generate publicity, good or bad; who can credibly paint a shadow or a halo around a politician's head. Politicians respond to people, the more of them the better. Activists who pursue political influence need the heartfelt, passionate support of a group of people.

★　★　★

One final form of political involvement for activists has been used with more success than any other in the past century. It was invented, strangely enough, by those who brought Prohibition to America. Their story is inspiring, but it also carries a large sign reading "Danger."

Everybody knows that Prohibition was a disastrous failure, but few know about the rampant success that preceded the failure. Of all activist movements in the history of the United States, none other showed such political sophistication nor gained so much raw political power as Prohibition. Often derided as naive moralists, the prohibitionists worked the political system with great skill. They were feared by senators and presidential candidates; they moved with ease and authority in the halls of Congress and in the White House. In the end they swept the field, passing an amendment to the U.S. Constitution that changed daily life for all Americans.

That success was primarily due to a single organization with its roots in Columbus, Ohio: the Anti-Saloon League (ASL). Though its success did not endure the test of time, its innovative techniques of influencing government have been copied by lobbying groups from all points on the political and reform compass. The ASL wrote the book on political-pressure groups.

To grasp how innovative the ASL was, it helps to contrast them to the two powerful prohibitionist groups that preceded them. One was the Prohibition Party, formed in 1869, four years after the end of the Civil War.

Five years later, the Woman's Christian Temperance Union (WCTU) joined the cause. It had a completely different origin: a spontaneous movement of Christian women who poured out of church prayer meetings to invade saloons and "joints." Thousands of women marched to the business district of their towns, fell to their knees in the mud or the sawdust and prayed. Through this technique they actually closed the doors of many saloons. The movement spread from Ohio throughout America, and when the immediate fire had ebbed, it organized itself into the WCTU. Women could not vote, so the WCTU operated as a semi-independent woman's auxiliary of the Prohibition Party.

For twenty years the WCTU and the Prohibition Party dominated the field of temperance. They represented a traditional American pattern of political organizing: democratic, grass-roots, taking stands on multiple issues and prone to organize as political parties. This approach was quite in tune with American politics, only it did not succeed in changing anything.

In 1894 a young minister named Howard Russell conceived of a completely different kind of organization: hierarchical and efficient, like the modern bureaucracies that American business was developing. Russell's group was organized on a nonpartisan basis for the single goal of eliminating the business interests that made alcohol available and attractive to Americans. If you think of the modern lobbying groups in American society—Bread for the World, the Right to Life Committee, Amnesty International, the National Association of Realtors—you will find the same basic characteristics. Though there is nominal grass-roots participation, and the operation relies on broad financial contributions, it is run by a small group of professional administrators. It does not compete with the existing political parties; it exists to influence them. And it depends on very skillful, almost scientific political pressure.

The ASL was run by a small group of men, mostly from Ohio, many of them Methodist pastors or laymen who had graduated from Oberlin College. Their names are redolent of small-town nineteenth-century America: Purley Baker, Ernest Cherrington, E. C. Dinwiddie, Wayne Wheeler, to name the most prominent.

They learned through trial and error how to create political battles that would mobilize people in the pews to support them—even if they lost. They learned how to work with the faithful so that pastors and denominational leaders would support the work and participate in local committees, even though they exercised no effective influence on the organization's decisions. Finances were gained from grass-roots offerings collected on special Sundays, as well as from rich contributors like John D. Rockefeller. Masses of literature were produced and distributed to the faithful. ASL agents made contact with all the political players in the state and kept careful notes of sympathetic and unsympathetic responses at all levels. They carefully classified voters and tailored messages to them at key times. Hundreds of agents worked in the field, building up support and raising money. Politicians crossed and double-crossed the ASL, but the organization remembered friends and enemies, and showed it could make a difference on election day. Politicians learned to fear them, first in Ohio, then in the whole nation.

The Prohibition Party criticized the ASL bitterly, calling them anonymous Republicans. What they meant was that they were not pure, as the Prohibition Party was pure; they were a support group for the impure Republicans, who typically competed for Prohibition Party votes.

In fact, however, a key breakthrough in Ohio came when the reigning Republicans nominated a wet candidate for governor and the ASL supported a dry Democrat, John Pattison. With the ASL's support, Pattison won even though every other state office was won by a Republican.

The ASL, having demonstrated their nonpartisan political power, made no attempt to have its allies appointed to political positions. They did not want to be directly involved in government but to stand outside and pressure the government—whatever party was involved—to take a stand against the liquor business.

Realists, too, they picked and chose when to fight. Beginning at the local level, they tried to make as many rural towns as possible dry. Then they worked at the county level. Eventually they succeeded at the state level. Though Ohio had many large cities with hard-drinking immigrant populations of Germans and Irish, the state went officially dry in 1918.

★ ★ ★

More and more localities went dry until, at the advent of national Prohibition, about half the population of the nation and two-thirds of its territory had already outlawed the trade in alcohol. To some extent this was due to the ASL's increasing skill in raising funds, convincing voters and influencing legislators. It was also due to a cultural reality: the United States had entered an era of optimistic reform, when the idea grew that government could and should improve the lives of ordinary people by controlling their diet, their living conditions and their working conditions. Regulatory agencies and food inspections grew during this time. Reform was on a roll. Prohibition fit the mood. If the government was going to protect America's health by ensuring food purity, it made sense to regulate alcohol like any dangerous drug or poison.

In 1913 the ASL made a historic decision to try for national Prohibition. It had always been the organization's stated objective, but they had described it the way Christians often describe the kingdom of God: something they hope to see, but who knows when or how. Only national legislation could penetrate the great eastern cities, where alcohol was widely accepted. If the decision was left to local voters, liquor would never disappear from New York. The ASL had always supported the idea of local option. National legislation, however, meant coercion over communities that did not support Prohibition. Local option went out the window.

There was a secret urgency to the national legislation. A careful analysis suggested that a growing population of new immigrants would change the political equation drastically after the census of 1920. ASL executives thought that if they didn't pass national Prohibition soon, they would never pass it.

Then World War I suddenly changed the mood of the country. Our boys were sacrificing their lives overseas; how could Americans carry on in dissolute living? When the supply of food became a serious wartime concern, how could the United States allow tons of grain to be diverted to beer and whiskey? Within a very short time, the unthinkable had occurred: Congress had ratified a constitutional amendment banning the production and sale of alcoholic beverages, and it was sent to the states. By early 1919, the necessary thirty-six states had given their approval. Prohibition was law.

★   ★   ★

In hindsight it is easy to see that the law was too flimsy to stand. It had been passed in a hurry, without a broad assent of the American people. Large areas of the country—the cities in particular—never agreed to Prohibition and made no attempt to obey or enforce it. The ASL, meanwhile, had used all its skill to pass legislation but had given very little thought to how to live with it.

Wayne Wheeler became the organization's chief spokesman in Washington, and he collaborated in a wretched, ham-handed approach to enforcement. In the process he violated the old ASL principle of not getting directly involved, for Wheeler loved the trappings of power and inserted himself in the administration at every point.

The mood changed. After World War I, America turned away from reform. The fundamentalist-modernist controversy and the *Scopes* trial cast a pall over religious causes.

It seems quite possible that Prohibition would have survived, even with poor enforcement and diminished support. In 1928 Herbert Hoover, a prohibitionist, and Al Smith, a well-known wet from New York, ran for president. Hoover won in a landslide, and prohibitionists heaved a sigh of relief. They thought they would have time to work out the obvious shortcomings of enforcement.

But they never saw the Great Depression coming. Within a very short time, Hoover's name became a curse word, and so did every policy associated with his name. Just as national Prohibition prospered from a certain kind of emotion associated with World War I, so it also suffered when those emotions changed. In the changed mood, the revulsion against national Prohibition also swung against local option. Soon there were few dry counties and almost no dry states.

The ASL was a smart, skillful political-pressure group. The techniques they developed worked miracles, and those techniques still work for political-pressure groups today. In the end, however, the ASL failed miserably. Perhaps the lesson is that they overreached. Or perhaps the lesson is that politics can accomplish only so much. Politics cannot make people do what they don't want to do; and it has a very limited ability to change hearts and minds. How much, then, can politics change the world?

★ ★ ★

Undoubtedly, much can be done through politics by those who want to change the world. However, politics is never as easy as idealists suppose.

Abolitionists who sought a grand coalition in the Free-Soil Party experienced profound disappointment. They realized that they had sold their principles for a squalid, semiracist mess—and not even to elect a single officer! Yet the Free-Soil Party contained the seeds of the Republican Party (which most abolitionists, burned by Free-Soil, wanted no part of), and that party played a large role in the end of slavery. What lesson can be drawn from this? Only that skepticism is in order when joining forces with other political forces—but not total skepticism. If you want to change the world, you can go there—but go with cautious realism.

Martin Luther King Jr. and his allies sought another kind of political power—dignified, behind-the-scenes influence. They were led to believe and wanted to believe that they gained secret power with the Kennedy administration. In reality they received promises that were broken, and almost nothing of substance. They learned the hard way to be wary of politicians who seem to be on your side. They also learned that access has value if at the same time you can create a ruckus on the ground.

Prohibitionists demonstrated how a disciplined pressure group can work to pass legislation intended to help millions of people. They did have votes, and they knew how to use them. And Prohibition worked: despite problems of enforcement, drunkenness and its attending evils dropped precipitously. However, Prohibition emphasizes the dangers of overreaching. Skill at political manipulation led to laws that went beyond the American consensus. Political success actually may have set the cause of temperance back because of the ultimate backlash. What lesson here? That politics can only do so much—and when it tries to do too much, it can leave a legacy of bitterness.

A case can be made for William Lloyd Garrison's approach. Through prophetic and stinging words, he stood on the sidelines and provoked America. His message got through. He didn't pretend to offer practical solutions to the problem of slavery. He spoke the truth about it. Others had to sort out the answers.

Prophets have an important place, I believe, but so do those who look for solutions. Many of them will be drawn toward political action. In democratic America, that impulse is almost unavoidable.

If activists take on politics, they need to maintain a community base outside of politics. If you live with both feet in a community that supports and understands your core values, then you will have something independent to stand on.

For example, Mary Nelson of Bethel New Life in Chicago mentions how important she finds the prayers of the elderly women in her church community. She knows that without the active support of a community of faith, she will be nothing more than a bossy woman. And stand-alone bossy women don't get far in the grit of city politics. Nelson gets respect from Chicago politicians because she stands with a community behind her.

Abolition triumphed because its moral point of view became America's moral point of view. Woman suffrage transformed the way most people see women. The civil rights movement's biggest achievement came in convincing Americans that racial prejudice is wrong.

Prohibition on the other hand failed because, despite great political skill, its leaders failed to convince Americans that alcohol was sufficiently evil to be banned. Today we live with a clear consensus that alcoholic beverages are normal.

The task of changing lives is beyond the power of politics. Politics can play a role, but only a limited role. The activist who is humble, who has limited and realistic expectations for what politics can accomplish, who keeps both feet in a supportive community outside politics and enters the political realm with the backing of an activist community, who remembers at all times that other arenas outside politics are at least equally significant in promoting changed lives—such an activist can contribute a lot, even in the political realm.

9

WHO IS AN ACTIVIST?

NOT LONG AGO I WAS TALKING WITH MY SON, Chase, about his desire to identify with the poor. He had been reading with great admiration about a Jesuit priest who lives in the garbage dumps of Manila. At the same time, Chase had just completed a year of living with an intentional Christian community in the poorest neighborhood of Pasadena, California. There he shared a roach-infested apartment so that he and his housemates—who worked a variety of day jobs—could make themselves available at all hours to the poor kids in the neighborhood.

With that year completed, Chase moved into a more "normal" apartment. He found it much easier on him. He could sleep. He could read. He works at World Vision, a global relief and development agency. The demands of work seem much more manageable now that he has a chance for peace and quiet at home. As he thinks about the future, about marriage and family and career, he finds the ideal of the Jesuit priest receding into the distance. But he doesn't want it to recede.

Chase thinks he ought to live like that Jesuit priest, but he is confronting the terrible gulf between his idealism and the realities of his own needs and wants. He feels guilty for failing to bridge that gulf.

"In this world there is no way to be totally right," I told him.

Chase said, "But I want to be right so badly!"

There are many young people like Chase—and older people too—who want to be right so badly. They have great ideals. They care passionately about the poor and want to give their lives to help. They care about God's creation, about justice and beauty and truth. I admire them tremendously, and I share their ideals, but I know they are going to be squeezed by life.

I referred Chase to Romans 3:21, which begins, "But now a righteousness from God, apart from law, has been made known." It helps to remember that ultimate rightness doesn't come from you and your brilliant, passionate choices. It comes from God and with his kingdom.

What would we really accomplish if we were to live the perfect justified life? Even if we could manage that (which we can't), we would not change the world. Living right is a good thing and an important thing, but the main thing is God's transformation of the world, which comes to earth from heaven. We get to follow and participate. That doesn't relieve us of responsibility, but it alleviates some of the anxiety of wanting to be totally right. Even when we fail, God will not fail.

★   ★   ★

I want to see this generation make a lasting difference. For that, we need activists who are both passionate and durable. Young people like Chase—will they participate in changing the world, not just for a year but for a lifetime? How many will last in their passion for the poor? How many will be effective? Thirty years from now, how many will you find keeping their ideals alive?

I don't necessarily mean enduring as a full-time, sold-out

activist. If everybody were a full-time activist, we would have no food to eat, because nobody would be out farming. No children would get an education, because no one would give their lives to teaching. We'd have no musicians, no musical instruments, no radios, no iPods.

We don't need everybody to live in the garbage dumps in Manila. We need some. We don't need everybody to spend their lives serving in the poorest neighborhood in Pasadena. We need some. We also need many who live more ordinary lives, occupied with family and work while carrying on in praying for activist movements that work for justice, giving to their financial support and lending Saturdays or evenings or vacations to their cause. They are activists too.

What we don't need are people who give their hearts to justice while they are in college, and then upon graduation discover investment banking and never again give a serious thought to their obligations to the needy. We don't need people to donate a year or two of youthful idealism and then forget it. We don't need burnout cases or cynical former idealists who tried to change the world and then discovered it was impossible.

Passionate yet durable: that kind of activist is born of wise and gracious community life. The burden of this book is that we can trace our heritage from a long line of activists who came before us. They have a lot to teach us. The wisdom of the past is the best ingredient I know for a solid future.

★ ★ ★

Through these chapters we have traced a sort of *Pilgrim's Progress* for people who want to change the world. Just as John Bunyan's classic allegory suggests that all Christians follow a foreseeable pathway, so in America the life of a would-be activist proceeds along a semipredictable arc.

It starts with truth. It would be a good idea for every would-be activist to ask herself or himself, what is the truth I want the world to live by? We can do without activism that is fueled only by fashionable opinions or the adrenaline of passionate activity.

By identifying his or her core truth, an activist can keep focused and discriminate between important battles and petty scrimmages. For example, if you are lying in front of earthmoving machines to prevent the building of a nuclear power plant, you should know why. Certainly it is not enough to say that you and all your friends hate nuclear power. You need a deeper truth to fuel your activism, such as this, perhaps: nuclear power is uniquely risky because of the very nature of its technology. (And thus you should be able to discuss some details of its unique dangers.)

Truth is or should be at the core of all efforts to change the world. That means the true activist is a witness, anxious to pass on truth to others. Genuine activism always has a truth message. It is not just an exercise in power.

As we saw early in this book, however, the first lesson of activism is that not everybody wants to listen to the truth. Many people do not care whether you are right or wrong; they will not be budged out of their preconceived and comfortable position.

So the real activist has to deal with frustration. The greatness of America (or any country) isn't actually so great. America puts up with inequity in the courts, children going hungry, children being eliminated from the womb. And not just America broadly speaking, but your neighbors, the members of your church, your representatives in Washington. Many just don't want you to bother them.

It would be a good idea for every would-be activist to ask, where do I place my hope? In human nature? In American democracy? In the progress of ideas? In God? We don't need activism that turns bitter and disgusted when it encounters resistance. We need activism that is fueled by an abiding hope.

Activists also discover the systemic nature of resistance. Not only are people stubbornly disinterested in truth, their stubbornness is sustained and strengthened by a social network: institutions, customs, habits of mind, economic interests, associations. All these work together to preserve the status quo.

Thus the real activist discovers that witnessing to the truth is not enough. You must have a strategy for shaking the system, and that strategy often involves pressure tactics. Protests, strikes and boycotts are designed to make people uncomfortable within the system. The trouble with pressure tactics is that they can become an end in themselves if activists lose sight of the big picture.

Pressure tactics don't change the world; they blow the whistle. Protests can grab people's attention so they will listen to the truth. Then the possibility of change begins—but only begins. Somebody has to follow behind the pressure tactics to see that practical change occurs. There always remains a great deal of work to do in dialogue and negotiation to enable real and lasting change.

Often that follow-up work lacks the sizzle of pressure tactics. Some would rather follow their adrenaline than buckle down to the mundane. We need activists who see the goal clearly and aren't led by mere excitement.

Activists engaged in pressure tactics get tired and dry. They grow bitter and burned-out partly because adrenaline is not enough. It would be good for every activist to ask what resources they have to sustain themselves. We need long-term, lively, loving people who don't get too high or too low. If they are prophets, we need them to last, not blow up like fireworks. Such endurance usually requires continued involvement in a sustaining community (not necessarily composed of activists). It requires a lifestyle that has room for rest, for relationships, for recreation and for restoration. (Reading, worship, prayer and meditation are some components.)

If the cause is held with great passion, the temptation toward violence will usually surface. It seems inconceivable in the beginning, but bombers and arsonists and dirty tricksters are a threat to every movement, no matter how nonviolent its stance. It would be good for every activist to ask what he or she has said, out loud, to make clear that violent or destructive tactics have no place in the movement. It would be a good idea for every activist movement to jump on shadowy comments that might harbor violent ideas, and to keep watch on people who might act on them. Violent acts can wreck movements before they have a chance to change the world.

★　★　★

Then comes politics. In America every reform movement will be drawn toward it because we are a people who instinctively trust our democracy and bring our causes to it. Even movements to reduce the scope of government work through government.

Activists often feel attracted to the single-issue third party that makes timeless gestures of purity and principle. Then, frustrated by the lack of results, many activists go on to other approaches.

Three are classic: joining forces with (partly) like-minded political factions to try to make a workable political coalition; trying to cultivate friends on the inside of government; or developing a sophisticated lobbying operation that can work the political system to manufacture change. All these approaches to politics—and there are many variations on them—have some success, but all of them will produce imperfect results. That is because reformers are idealists, motivated by truth, while politics is the art of realism, motivated by power and dealing in compromises. Politicians pay attention to actual voters, with their narrow, selfish interests, whereas activists think of the world that should be. Politicians aim to win elections; activists aim to change the world.

We do not want activists to become mere political operatives, slaves to the faction's competitive aims. We want activists to inject idealism and creativity into the political realm and not be swallowed up in it. In order to do that, activists need to have a base community, independent of the political world, engaged in solving the grass-roots problems they care about. They need a community that can sustain their idealism and their hope. They need a community that can exercise influence apart from the political system.

★ ★ ★

I can't hide the fact that an activist's life is fraught with frustration. The historical record is full of it. As I describe the predictable arc of an activist's life, repeatedly I have to say that it doesn't always work out the way the activist hoped.

A realistic question is, who needs this? If the activist's pathway involves large doses of disillusionment and discouragement, with multiple temptations to self-righteousness, violence or political trivialization, who wants to change the world? The pathway I have described is not bordered by flower beds and shade trees. It is a desert land. Who would want to follow this road? And why?

As a Christian I give this answer: the kingdom of God, which Jesus Christ proclaimed as breaking into our world.

I do not mean every activist must be a Christian (though I do think every Christian should be in some sense an activist). A great many wonderful reformers and activists are emphatically *not* Christians and would be repelled by the idea that they must be.

I mean that this idea of the kingdom of God underlies the reforming impulse in all Western societies. And it is more than an idea. I believe the kingdom of God is growing within the structure of our world. Those who want to change the world are responding to cues from a deeper reality, whether East or West. The kingdom of God is really happening, and we feel it. We feel the discrepancy between what is and what ought to be.

Many people have thought Jesus was saying something vague and nice when he talked about the kingdom of God, on the order of "all we need is love." They have imagined him urging people to look at the world through spiritual glasses, seeing God everywhere.

But that is not what Jesus was saying. He spoke quite realistically. The kingdom of God meant that things are being put right, the way God promised.

Jesus not only announced it, he acted on it. Wherever he went and with whomever he talked, a little bit of the world set right could be seen. Jesus also began to gather a corps of followers and train them to act as his lieutenants. He recruited them to help announce and enact the new reality.

This is the very nature of the universe, according to Christian faith: it belongs to its maker, who loves it, who wants it to be as lovely as he made it. The whole cosmos groans in a kind of therapeutic pain as it endures this discrepancy between how it is and how it was intended to be. And the time is here to put it right. We are called to join in the changing. This is a moral vision based not on law or coercion, but on love.

Jesus said that the most basic demands of life can be put simply: love God, and love your neighbor. Love is at the basis of all activism that is worth anything: love of people, love of God, love of God's world. That is why we take on the discouraging business of changing the world—because of love. We do not generate this love in ourselves; it exists in the world apart from us. This love will sustain us if we recognize it for what it is: a gift from God.

ACKNOWLEDGMENTS

IT WAS RALPH WINTER WHO QUITE accidentally started me on this project many years ago by recommending that I learn about the Tappan brothers of New York City. One thing led to another. I want to thank Andy Le Peau and all the staff at IVP who encouraged me to write this book. Andy has been a helpful editor and counselor throughout. Others read the manuscript and made useful comments, many of which changed the book substantially. They are: Harold Fickett, Preston Jones, Mark Labberton, Chase Stafford, Philip Yancey and John Wilson—faithful friends. My wife, Popie, has been the most faithful friend of all, giving me good editorial advice and wonderful encouragement.

NOTES

Chapter 1: How Do We Change the World?

page 16   Years ago I wrote: Tim Stafford, "Ron Sider's Unsettling Crusade," *Christianity Today*, April 27, 1992, pp. 18-22.

page 20   That's part of the real-life penalty: Tim Stafford, "The Pastor Without a Paycheck," *Christianity Today*, April 2003, pp. 90-93.

page 20   On assignment: Tim Stafford, "Inside Crisis Pregnancy Centers," *Christianity Today*, August 17, 1992, pp. 20-24.

Chapter 2: Starting with Truth

page 37   "If there is not timber": Louis Filler, *Crusade Against Slavery: Friends, Foes, and Reforms, 1820-1860* (Algonac, Mich.: Reference Publications, 1986), p. 87.

pages 39-41   We have met together: The 1833 Declaration of Sentiments can be found on a number of websites, such as <http://usinfo.state.gov/usa/infousa/facts/democrac/18.htm>.

Chapter 3: Meeting Resistance

page 43   Arthur Tappan: Bertram Wyatt-Brown, *Lewis Tappan and the Evangelical War Against Slavery* (Baton Rouge: Louisiana State University Press, 1969), p. 152.

page 44   "unconstitutional and wicked": Merton L. Dillon, *The Abolitionists: The Growth of a Dissenting Minority* (New York: W. W. Norton, 1974), p. 90.

page 46   They met: Of the many accounts of the Lane debates, the most thorough is Lawrence Thomas Lesick, *The Lane Rebels: Evangelicalism and Antislavery in Antebellum America* (Metuchen, N.J.: Scarecrow Press, 1980).

page 47   highly influential book: Theodore D. Weld, *American Slavery As It Is: Testimony of a Thousand Witnesses* (New York: American Anti-Slavery Society, 1839).

page 49   "If you want to": Lesick, *Lane Rebels*, p. 94.

page 51   "The great body": Gilbert H. Barnes and Dwight L. Dumond, eds., *The Letters of Theodore Dwight Weld, Angelina Grimke Weld, and Sarah Grimke, 1822-1844* (Gloucester, Mass.: Peter Smith, 1965), p. 796.

page 51   "The Anti Slavery heart": Ibid., p. 969.

page 52   "the movement to abolish": Dillon, *Abolitionists,* p. 228.

Chapter 4: Pressure Tactics

page 65   "We, the disinherited": Charles Marsh, *The Beloved Community: How Faith Shapes Social Justice, from the Civil Rights Movement to Today* (New York: BasicBooks, 2005), p. 23.

page 65   "if we are wrong": Taylor Branch, *Parting the Waters: America in the King Years, 1954-63* (New York: Simon & Schuster, 1988), p. 141.

page 65   Here is the complete list: Marsh, *Beloved Community,* p. 24; and David J. Garrow, *Bearing the Cross: Martin Luther King, Jr., and the Southern Christian Leadership Conference* (New York: W. Morrow, 1986), pp. 21-22.

page 66   "willingness to suffer": Marsh, *Beloved Community,* p. 25.

page 67   "We are committed": Ibid., p. 41.

pages 73-74 "SNCC went cosmic": Ibid., p. 113.

page 80   "Don't get panicky": Branch, *Parting the Waters,* p. 166.

Chapter 5: Staying Power

page 81   Other student volunteers: Taylor Branch, *Parting the Waters: America in the King Years, 1954-63* (New York: Simon & Schuster, 1988), p. 325.

page 83   "We can't let": Ibid., p. 497.

page 83   Moses had clasped: Ibid., p. 500.

page 84   Historian Taylor Branch tells: Ibid., p. 634.

page 85   "We can't protect": Ibid., p. 921.

page 87   "From now on": Ibid, p. 590.

page 90   I thought about: John Lewis with Michael D'Orso, *Walking with the Wind: A Memoir of the Movement* (New York: Simon & Schuster, 1998), p. 368.

page 90   It hurt: Ibid., p. 373.

page 91   "As I rode": Ibid., p. 374.

page 91   "Without prayer": Charles Marsh, *God's Long Summer* (Princeton, N.J.: Princeton University Press, 1997), jacket blurb.

page 93   In *The Lane Rebels:* Thomas Lesick, *The Lane Rebels: Evangelicalism and Antislavery in Antebellum America* (Metuchen, N.J.: Scarecrow Press, 1980), pp. 235-36.

page 94   "Let every abolitionist": Robert H. Abzug, *Passionate Liberator: Theodore Dwight Weld and the Dilemma of Reform* (New York: Oxford University Press, 1980), p. 148.

page 97   "in a thousand years": Bertram Wyatt-Brown, *Lewis Tappan and the Evangelical War Against Slavery* (Baton Rouge: Louisiana State University Press, 1969), p. 177.

page 98   "After many years": Ibid., p. 178.

Chapter 6: The Seduction of Violence

page 106   "the men would not": Robert Smith Bader, *Prohibition in Kansas: A History* (Lawrence: University Press of Kansas, 1986), p. 136.

page 108   "All felt that the state": Ibid., p. 133.

page 108   "Moral suasion!": Ibid., p. 140.

page 116   She was given a hero's welcome: Ann Hegedorn, *Beyond the River: The Untold Story of the Heroes of the Underground Railroad* (New York: Simon & Schuster, 2002), pp. 123-43; James M. McPherson, *Battle Cry of Freedom: The Civil War Era* (New York: Oxford University Press, 1988), p. 146.

page 119   "We will be compelled": McPherson, *Battle Cry of Freedom,* p. 146.

page 119   "Would not one": Bertram Wyatt-Brown, *Lewis Tappan and the Evangelical War Against Slavery* (Baton Rouge: Louisiana State University Press, 1969), p. 333.

Chapter 7: Party Politics and the Prophetic Alternative

page 128   "a covenant with death": Louis Filler, *Crusade Against Slavery: Friends, Foes, and Reforms, 1820-1860* (Algonac, Mich.: Reference Publications, 1986), p. 259.

page 129   "A great many": Merton L. Dillon, *The Abolitionists: The Growth of a Dissenting Minority* (New York: W. W. Norton, 1974), p. 146.

page 130   "as fast as *we*": Ibid.

page 133   "the existing parties": Thomas R. Pegram, *Battling Demon Rum: The*

Struggle for Dry America, 1800-1933 (Chicago: Ivan R. Dee, 1998), p. 51.

page 134   "give the otherwise ignored": Rick Gaber, "Third Parties: What They're For and What They Do" <http://freedomkeys.com/3rdpartieswhatforb.htm>.

page 136   "that under the pressure": Hugh Davis, *Joshua Leavitt, Evangelical Abolitionist* (Baton Rouge: Louisiana State University Press, 1990), p. 244.

page 136   "The Liberty party": Richard H. Sewell, *Ballots for Freedom: Antislavery Politics in the United States, 1837-1860* (New York: W. W. Norton, 1976), p. 153.

page 137   "tone of candor": Davis, *Joshua Leavitt*, p. 247.

page 138   "We have gained everything": Ibid., p. 246.

Chapter 8: Applying Political Pressure

page 144   Taylor Branch recounts: Taylor Branch, *Parting the Waters: America in the King Years, 1954-63* (New York: Simon & Schuster, 1988), p. 429.

page 149   "Today I sat": Ibid., p. 773.

page 150   "The United States is concerned": Ibid., p. 791.

Author and subject indexes are available online at www.ivpress.com.